# Help Lord, I'm Sinking

## LESSONS FROM MY ROCKING BOAT

### CAROLE MAYHALL

D0062520

NAVPRESS
BRINGING TRUTH TO LIFE
NavPress Publishing Group
P.O. Box 35001, Colorado Springs, Colorado 80935

The Navigators is an international Christian organization. Our mission is to reach, disciple, and equip people to know Christ and to make Him known through successive generations. We envision multitudes of diverse people in the United States and every other nation who have a passionate love for Christ, live a lifestyle of sharing Christ's love, and multiply spiritual laborers among those without Christ.

NavPress is the publishing ministry of The Navigators. NavPress publications help believers learn biblical truth and apply what they learn to their lives and ministries. Our mission is to stimulate spiritual formation among our readers.

© 1997 by Carole Mayhall
Library of Congress Catalog Card Number: 97-31605
ISBN 1-57683-075-6

Cover design by Raul Colon / Vickie Morgan Associates

Some of the anecdotal illustrations in this book are true to life and are included with the permission of the persons involved. All other illustrations are composites of real situations, and any resemblance to people living or dead is coincidental.

Unless otherwise identified, all Scripture quotations in this publication are taken from the HOLY BIBLE: NEW INTERNATIONAL VERSION ® (NIV®). Copyright © 1973, 1978, 1984 by International Bible Society. Used by permission of Zondervan Publishing House. All rights reserved. Other versions used include: the New American Standard Bible (NASB), © The Lockman Foundation 1960, 1962, 1963, 1968, 1971, 1972, 1973, 1975, 1977; the Revised Standard Version Bible (RSV), copyright 1946, 1952, 1971, by the Division of Christian Education of the National Council of the Churches of Christ in the USA, used by permission, all rights reserved; The New Testament in Modern English (PH), J. B. Phillips Translator, © J. B. Phillips 1958, 1960, 1972, used by permission of Macmillan Publishing Company; The Living Bible (TLB), copyright © 1971, used by permission of Tyndale House Publishers, Inc., Wheaton, IL 60189, all rights reserved; The New English Bible (NEB), © 1961, 1970, The Delegates of the Oxford University Press and The Syndics of the Cambridge University Press; the Amplified New Testament (AMP), © The Lockman Foundation 1954, 1958; the New King James Version (NKJV), copyright © 1979, 1980, 1982, 1990, Thomas Nelson Inc., Publishers; and the King James Version (KJV).

Mayhall, Carole.
     Help Lord, I'm sinking : lessons from my rocking boat / Carole Mayhall.
        p.   cm.
     Includes bibliographical references.
     ISBN 1-57683-075-6
1. Christian life.  2. Mayhall, Carole.  I. Title.
     BV4501.2.M423     1998
     248.4–dc21                           97-31605
                                                  CIP

Printed in the United States of America

1 2 3 4 5 6 7 8 9 10 11 12 13 14 15 / 00 99 98 97

# Contents

*To Joye Hoekzema Server,*
*now at home in heaven.*
*She faced*
*life with laughter,*
*death with courage and grace . . .*
*And, in the process, taught those of us around her precious*
*lessons concerning both.*

A special thanks to all at NavPress who not only had a vision for this book, but who took the ball and ran with it!

I *especially* want to thank Joanne Heim who, during a difficult storm in her own life, managed to do a lion's share of work on this project. *Thanks, Joanne!*

# Introduction

Help Lord . . .
Help Lord . . .
Help Lord . . .

The phone rang imperatively, and I dashed in from the yard, trowel in my mud-caked hand. My sister's voice sounded trembly and far away.

"I just got home from the doctor," she said. "You know I've been having pains in my head and chest for a few weeks, but the doctor couldn't find anything wrong. Today I noticed a lump on my neck, and when I went in to be checked, the doctor took another X-ray and sent me to a specialist. After his examination, he told me I should enter the hospital immediately. He thinks it's serious."

I sank to the floor, clutching the phone, fighting the sinking feeling inside me. "What do you mean, *serious*?"

"He wouldn't come right out and say. Just that he would advise immediate hospitalization and it was 'very serious.' I said I couldn't go in right away. I've just got too many things to finish. We're redecorating the apartment upstairs, my back room is a mess, and. . . . "

"Oh, Joye!" My voice was choked with tears. "Those things aren't important. Please do what the doctor advises and let's find out what it is."

As I hung up the phone that June afternoon in 1977, panic

poked a gaping hole in my peace. "Lord, not my sister! Just two months ago You took Mom. And Joye is such a vivacious, loving wife and mother — so vital. She is growing spiritually and serving You with all her heart. I love her so. Not Joye, Lord, *please.*"

The next four days were a nightmare of tests and more tests. We anxiously kept in touch twice a day by phone. I didn't want to be home in Colorado when she was in an Indiana hospital, but there was nothing to be done until the tests were concluded. For me, those days were filled with tears. Jack, my husband, spent much time just comforting me. I made reservations to fly out to be with Joye the day after her biopsy.

Then the diagnosis was confirmed — cancer. Joye had acute lymphatic leukemia, a rare disease among adults. My father died only six days after receiving an identical diagnosis at the age of fifty-seven. The reality of Joye's illness destroyed my last vestiges of self-control and unleashed a torrent of crippling fear and pain.

I was a basket case! I couldn't speak without crying. I couldn't think about blueberry jam, home-canned pickles, or antiques, all of which were intimately connected in my mind with my sister. And I was flying to her the next day to *help.* How could I help in the condition I was in?

The night was warmly soft as I slipped out onto our small upstairs porch. I needed help desperately.

"Lord, help me," I pleaded. "I need You more now than I've ever needed You. I need Your strength, Your grace, Your comfort. You *promised* to be my strength when I am weak, and I am claiming that promise right now."

I stopped and took a deep breath as God's mantle of peace settled over me. My flood of words suddenly evaporated along with my tears, and I went inside to bed — and to sleep.

The next morning I flew to Indiana, but what a difference! Instead of turbulence, there was peace. Instead of shakiness, God's strength. Instead of anxiety, comfort and grace.

Joye was death-gray and perspiring when I entered her hospital room. Blue-black circles framed eyes closed in weariness and pain. A white bandage encased her neck where the biopsy was performed. The day before, I would have started weeping again. Now I felt a comforting strength that was obviously not mine.

During the week that followed, even while holding Joye's hands during an excruciatingly painful spinal tap, my heart was supernaturally, inexplicably *calm.*

For Joye, and for all of us who were with her every waking moment—her husband Fred, daughter Melody, and myself—there was abundant, abounding grace. Not just a little grace, not just enough to "squeak through" those agonizing days, but a full, triumphant, glorious grace—a grace spelled j-o-y. A pervading peace made it a week of glory. God's strength lifted our hearts in praise. It was a week of miracles in all our hearts.

Every year when I was a student at Wheaton College our president, Dr. V. Raymond Edman, would give a chapel message on the theme, "Not Somehow, But Triumphantly." I thought of this many times during that week, for God was measuring out His grace, not just somehow, but in a truly *triumphant* way.

During the next months, the words of Psalm 90:12 kept nudging me: "Teach us to number our days that we may present to Thee a heart of wisdom" (NASB). I began to pray, "Lord, that is what I desire with all my heart. Joye has an idea of how many days she has here on earth. But I don't. I need You to teach *me* to number my days, be they few or many, that I might present to You a *heart of wisdom.*"

That prayer sent me on a search to discover what God's wisdom really is, which I wrote about in *Lord, Teach Me Wisdom.* But the boat of my life continued to be buffeted by many storms, both big and small, including the tidal wave of Joye's death. I felt overwhelmed, off balance, and battered. The lessons of God were deep and precious, and so I wrote *Lord of My Rocking Boat.* Then, about a year after Joye went to heaven, God stilled the storms for a time and filled my life with peace. I began to study what qualities God wants His children to be "filled with"—even "filled to overflowing." Thus the final book of the events surrounding Joye's going home came into being as *Filled to Overflowing.*

I'm grateful that the editors of NavPress offered to combine much of the material of these three books into the volume you hold in your hand. My prayer is that some of the lessons God taught me along my journey will help show you the greatness and glory of our Lord—through the storms, yes, but also *through the sunlight.*

Help Lord . . .

Help Lord . . .

Help Lord . . .

PART ONE

# Lord, Teach Me Wisdom

. . . I'm Sinking

# CHAPTER ONE

# Wisdom, Knowledge, and Understanding

Help Lord . . .
Help Lord . . .
Help Lord . . .

"Help, Lord. What do we do now?" I prayed. In two days Joye's doctor would begin a course of treatment that, once started, would be irreversible. Was it the right one?

Her doctor, a leukemia specialist, told us honestly that he'd treated only one other adult patient with the same rare form of the disease. We consulted another specialist, who advocated a radically different form of treatment.

The time for making a decision was short. We received conflicting advice—both to leave her in the hands of the nearby doctor and to fly her to a cancer clinic elsewhere immediately. We were all so caught up in our own emotions, it was impossible to be objective or calm.

Doing something—anything—seemed imperative. I telephoned four Christian doctor friends and asked them this question: "I need some advice from you first as a Christian, then as a husband, and lastly as a doctor. If your wife had acute lymphatic leukemia, what would you choose as the course of treatment?"

My father died of leukemia twenty years before Joye was diagnosed. Vast research had been done and much knowledge gained since that time. But a great deal still needed to be learned. I found that there are almost as many variations of treatment as there are hospitals treating the disease. One well-known clinic tried to kill the disease by massive doses of new experimental medicines given mainly in one week's time. Another spread part of the same treatment over an extended period. One theory said that leukemia cells "hide" in the brain during a remission period, and it suggested radiation to the brain to kill the cancer cells; another said this treatment was no longer considered feasible for adults. The variety of advice was confusing.

My doctor friends expressed concern and support. Three of the four said they would keep their wives at home for treatment nearby. The ultimate decision, of course, rested with Fred and Joye.

At that moment we were frustrated with the lack of knowledge in the medical field concerning this disease. Without precise knowledge, deciding what to do was beyond human capability.

Knowledge must come before wisdom. You have to know about something (knowledge) before you can take a proper course of action (wisdom). The dictionary defines knowledge as "knowing something with familiarity gained through experience or association" and "the fact or condition of being aware of something." Wisdom is defined as the "ability to discern inner qualities and relationships, insight; good sense, judgment."

I remembered that King Solomon asked God for *both* wisdom *and* knowledge (see 2 Chronicles 1:10), and God commended Solomon for his choice. In fact, God said it was such a good choice that He would give Solomon not only wisdom and knowledge, but also the riches and honor he hadn't asked for (2 Chronicles 1:12).

In this beautiful account we find that wisdom and knowledge are integrally associated with understanding and discernment. The same story recorded in 1 Kings 3 tells us that Solomon asked for "an understanding heart" to judge the people (verse 9). God rephrased Solomon's request in His reply. He said that because Solomon asked for "discernment [or hearing] to understand justice, behold I have given you a wise and discerning heart" (verses 11-12, NASB).

If ever we needed discernment, we needed it to decide which course of treatment was best for Joye. And while our human knowledge of this rare form of cancer was extremely limited, God's wisdom and knowledge was total! He led Fred and Joye to choose treatment by the doctor close to them, the doctor who had treated only one other adult with the disease. But they prayed, with many others, that this doctor would be given wisdom to use the method of treatment that would be best for her. We saw God do miracles in guiding that doctor. Let me tell you about just one.

Joye was not only weak and ill but also extremely sensitive to pain from so many injections, blood tests, and her biopsy. In order to find out if the disease was in remission, another bone marrow test had to be administered, along with the first injection into her spine of a chemotherapy drug—both tremendously painful procedures that had to be done without an anesthetic. We began to pray the week before the test and treatment that God would deliver her from fear and give her strength. He did much more than that!

On a Tuesday morning, two nurses stood by the doctor to hold Joye still during the bone marrow test. But they weren't needed. As the doctor drilled through the chest bone, Joye was supposed to feel a "drawing sensation" when the needle penetrated the marrow. But God so sustained and protected her that she not only felt *no* pain, she didn't even feel the needle in the marrow. The doctor even had to wiggle it around a bit to be sure he had placed it correctly! As he proceeded to the spinal injection, which was to be the first of four weekly injections, God again blocked the pain.

We were thankful and thrilled to see what God did. The next week we prayed that God again would block the pain of the injection. He didn't. Instead, it took the doctor three attempts before the spinal needle penetrated. Joye had a difficult time of it.

"Why, Lord?" I asked. "I know You give only good gifts to Your children. We knew last week was a good gift, but can this be good?"

As we learned, God doesn't always show us the "whys" of our trials. Some questions will be answered only in heaven when we learn more about His purposes. But this time, God enabled us to catch a glimpse of what He had done. That day, Joye's doctor decided to cancel the two remaining injections—a decision we knew resulted from the difficulty of the second injection. We could see this was God's way of giving Joye's doctor wisdom to know how to treat her. She went into a strong, yearlong remission; in her case, the four doses might have been too much.

Many times in my life I have clung to the promise in James 1:5: "If any of you lacks wisdom, he should ask God, who gives generously to all without finding fault, and it will be given to him." My wisdom is minimal at best. I need His wisdom daily—even hourly.

God tells us, however, to increase our *knowledge* so we will gain wisdom. "A wise man will hear and increase in learning," Solomon said (Proverbs 1:5, NASB). Knowledge is to be sought diligently!

When I read Proverbs 2:1-6, the verbs vied for my attention:

> "My son, if you will *receive* my sayings, And *treasure* my commandments within you, Make your ear attentive to wisdom, *Incline* your heart to understanding; For if you *cry* for discernment, Lift your voice for understanding; If you *seek* her as silver, And *search* for her as for hidden treasures; Then you will discern the fear of the LORD, And discover the knowledge of God. For the LORD gives wisdom; From His mouth come knowledge and understanding." (NASB, emphasis added)

We are to *pursue* wisdom and *search* for knowledge. And yet the knowledge and wisdom, and even the search for them, are all wrapped up in *God Himself.* We are to *search* for wisdom, but the Lord *gives* it (verse 6). We are to *cry* for it, but the fear of the Lord *is* wisdom and knowledge (Proverbs 1:7).

⑥

During those initial weeks of Joye's illness, God gave guidance, wisdom, and abundant peace. However, one dark morning I felt the edges of my strength begin to crumble. Peace started to fade into the horizon of pain. I realised that God had given me a hundred-pound sack of His grace to get through the first weeks of Joye's illness. But that day I awakened fearful and weak again, on the verge of tears. I had used up the last of the hundred-pound sackful. What should I do? How could I keep going?

And then I remembered: "Daily will I help thee."

God's grace had not been used up. It is fathomless—inexhaustible. In the preceding weeks I didn't have the time or energy to call continually upon Him for His grace. God knew that, and so He gave me an abundant supply. But now God wanted the closeness of my moment-by-moment dependence so that He could freely give and give and give again. I would remain weak if I refused to depend on Him and ask Him for the grace to be at peace, to be joyful, and to be calm.

I prayed then, "Oh, Lord, thank You for Your hundred-pound sacks of grace. But thank You, too, for the daily measure, always sufficient."

Understanding is a course God knows I need, and this insight into God's various ways of giving me grace helped to open the eyes of my heart. I'm also seeing how frequently God uses His servants to demonstrate something about understanding.

We were enjoying a few days of rest and study at our friends' beautiful summer home. Not being accustomed to their new electric range (mine took ages to warm up), I set some oil for popcorn on a burner and went into the living room to tell Jack something. It was only a moment, but upon returning to the kitchen I discovered the oil had burst into flames and the copper hood over the stove was on fire! I screamed for Jack and reached for the pan and a towel at the same time. Putting the pan down hastily in the sink, I frantically beat at the flaming hood as Jack reached the kitchen to help. In a moment the fire was out, but the damage had been done. The beautiful copper hood was no longer beautiful. It was black. Soot had turned the ceiling gray and greasy.

The next morning we tried to wash the ceiling and walls but only succeeded in leaving a line of dirt where we had washed, and the soot wasn't coming off completely anyway. I was depressed as I phoned my friend Lois to tell her what had happened, more unhappy than if it had been my own kitchen.

Lois's lilting voice was reassuring and sympathetic, and I had to stop right there and thank God for Christian friends. It was as if Lois and her husband had been able to put themselves in our place and truly understand.

Throughout the Bible we see that the God of wisdom is completely understanding. He sympathizes with our weaknesses and is merciful and faithful.[1] He can put Himself in our place to understand us because He was one of us.

I look at my God who totally understands, and I worship.

But then I look at myself. And when I look at myself, I get discouraged. So many times I am not understanding—of people, of situations, of spiritual truths. So the question comes to me time and time again: How can I become an understanding person—understanding like my friend Lois, but even more than that, understanding like God?

Before I can answer, I have to know what understanding is.

To understand means "to grasp the meaning of," "to grasp the reasonableness of," or "to show a sympathetic or tolerant attitude toward something." My own definition is simply, "the ability to put yourself in the place of another."

Jack has demonstrated this to me throughout the years, but one incident comes to mind. We were driving in the car one day when the sun came out from under a large bank of clouds and I automatically reached for my sunglasses in my purse.

Suddenly all my nerves came to attention as I frantically searched for my purse. Nothing! We were on our way home after a week's vacation, and I said desperately, "Jack! I can't find my purse!"

He pulled quickly to the side of the road and we began our hunt through the car. I thought, *Not much cash, but many credit cards, keys, driver's license. . . .*

"I must have left it at McDonald's when we stopped for lunch. What a silly thing to do!" I chided myself.

Instead of saying, "Yes, it was a stupid thing to do. How come you can't remember your purse? Why did you take it in anyway?" he said, "I'm so sorry. I know how you feel."

We pulled off the interstate into the first filling station. Some husbands would have slouched in the car and said, "Well, hurry up and call. We haven't got all day."

Jack quietly took charge. He called McDonald's and cushioned the news that nothing had been turned in there.

As we drove the rest of the way home, we prayed about it together. We had seen God help us find contact lenses lost in sawdust by our daughter, Lynn, and we had seen Him take care of our possessions and guard our safety; we knew He could care for one brown purse.

Some husbands would have given their wives instructions:

"When we get home you'll have to call the credit card companies. Tomorrow you can call the locksmith." Jack said, "I love you. We'll take care of it."

When we returned home, Jack called a tennis resort where we had stopped. Then he checked back with McDonald's once more before beginning the credit card calling. To our great relief, the purse had been found intact and was in their safe. We thanked God for once again protecting us.

That evening, as I reflected on the incident, two things were prominent: an overwhelming love for a husband who was so kind, and a realization of Jack's understanding. Jack had put himself in my shoes and truly understood. Because of this, he acted in a loving and considerate way.

The ability to put yourself in the place of another—to comprehend how he or she is feeling—is a great part of understanding. Lois and Dean had been able to do this when we blackened their lovely kitchen. Jack had done this when I lost my purse. God does this *every moment of our lives.*

The origin of the word *understand* is interesting:

Five hundred years ago one could have talked about "understanding (standing under) a tree in a rainstorm." As one of Shakespeare's characters put it, "Why, stand under and understand is all one." Today, however, only the figurative meaning is used, and to understand means to have a comprehension or awareness of something or its meaning (as if one knew something from the bottom up, from having stood under it).[2]

I like that! Understanding is to "see things from the bottom up . . . to stand under"—to really put yourself in the place of another, and to comprehend. Understanding is not just close kin to wisdom but an integral part of it. Solomon said, "Wisdom is in the presence of the one who has understanding" (Proverbs 17:24, NASB).

On the one hand, it is apparent that the Lord gives us understanding and wisdom. "For the LORD gives wisdom; from His mouth come knowledge and understanding" (Proverbs 2:6). On the other hand, I am to seek His knowledge so that I may have understanding, for "the knowledge of the Holy One is understanding" (Proverbs 9:10, NASB).

The truth seen from God's side shows that He gives wisdom when we pray for it, and when we know Christ, who is wisdom. Paul prayed for the Christians at Ephesus "that the God of our Lord Jesus Christ, the Father of glory, may give unto you the spirit of wisdom and revelation in the knowledge of him: The eyes of your understanding being enlightened" (Ephesians 1:17-18, KJV).

The truth from our side reveals that we must search for wisdom as for hidden treasures (look again at Proverbs 2:1-5).

While studying Proverbs, I discovered I couldn't separate knowledge, wisdom, and understanding into component parts. Every time I thought I had it figured out, a verse would erase the distinctions. "The fear of the LORD is the beginning of knowledge" we read in Proverbs 1:7. But in Proverbs 9:10 we learn, "The fear of the LORD is the beginning of wisdom, and knowledge of the Holy One is understanding." And in Proverbs 15:33, "The fear of the LORD teaches a man wisdom." These characteristics are unique, but like flour, water, and yeast combined to form bread, once baked they cannot be separated. My mind needed to examine the separate ingredients before digesting the whole loaf.

After meditating on these truths, I concluded that knowledge of God—heart knowledge that comes through searching the Word and praying—results in God *giving* wisdom, and with knowledge and wisdom come understanding. If I seek knowledge of God in His Word and in my everyday happenings, if I search for His wisdom as for hidden treasures, understanding should be a natural, growing thing in my life—a byproduct of the other two. Understanding is all wrapped up in letting the God of understanding fill my life with Himself. As my roots "go down deep into the soil of God's marvelous love" (Ephesians 3:17, LB), as I see the full extent of the love of Christ, then I shall be filled up with God Himself. My part is to search for His treasures and stay open to His filling. His part is to give me His understanding and wisdom.

*Father God, I need Your help in this. Please give me a heart to know You . . . the discipline to seek You. . . . a hunger to understand Your every word. Thank You. Amen.*

## FOR REFLECTION

1. Why must knowledge precede wisdom?
2. Are there areas in your life right now where you need wisdom?
3. How can you search for God's wisdom this week and apply it to those areas of your life?

# CHAPTER TWO

# Knowing the God of Wisdom

Help Lord . . .
Help Lord . . .
Help Lord . . .

She stood with her husband and tall son in the middle of a Brazilian shopping center. Crowds pressed around them, but to her, they were alone. Their attempts to communicate failed against the language barrier.

A silent, desperate prayer tore from her heart. "Lord, what are we to do? The plane leaves in a few hours for the jungles of the Amazon. Even the people who speak some English cannot understand that we need contact solution for Bobby's eyes. You know that with his eye disease, he *has* to have that solution. But no one understands us. Help us, *please*."

Americans alone. She had stopped several Brazilians, but even those who knew some English were unable to translate "contact solution," and the pharmacists were unable to comprehend her need.

As she prayed, a well-dressed Brazilian came toward her and she made one more faltering attempt. "Sir, do you speak English?" she asked.

He stopped abruptly and smiled. "Yes, I do. May I help you?"

The next half hour was incredible. He was a minister in the Brazilian government, with an important cabinet meeting in thirty minutes. Not only could he understand their need, he offered to drive them to a doctor who was a contact lens specialist. When a hurried trip across town found the office closed, he took them to the only place in Brasilia where the particular solution could be obtained — the pharmacy of the medical center. There the Brazilian minister phoned the doctor at his home to check the type of solution, purchased it, and then refused to be repaid by the Americans. Insisting that he still had time to make his meeting, he drove them back to the shopping center to catch a bus to the airport. When they thanked him, he replied, "I have been waiting several years for this opportunity. When I was in the United States a few years ago, someone was especially kind to me, and I have been looking for an opportunity to return that kindness to an American ever since."

God's timing is incredible!

One December, Jack and I were praying about whether I should accompany him on a business trip to Germany the following April. At long last it seemed there were no obstacles. Our daughter was married, and we had saved enough so that I could go on the trip — something we had been looking forward to for some time. As we prayed about it, we received a very definite "no" from God. Truthfully, I was upset to think God would say no when we had planned this for so long. I couldn't quite understand it because I know God delights to delight us. But He said no.

After Jack's plans were finalized, I was asked to speak at a women's conference in Michigan during the time he would be away, so I made plans to visit my sister and mother just prior to the conference.

As I walked in from church on a Sunday, the day before I was to fly to Michigan, the phone was ringing. It was my sister. "Mother has had a massive stroke," she said. "The doctor says you should come as soon as possible."

I already had my ticket; it was just a matter of changing the flight. I already had a person to come and stay in our home; she just had to come one night early. I already had a clear schedule. God had seen to that.

But He didn't stop there. Lynn and Tim, our daughter and her husband, who lived in Champaign, Illinois, just "happened" to be in Chicago that weekend. They were able to meet my plane, drive me to Michigan, and be the wonderful support that Jack couldn't be during this difficult time.

Arriving at my sister's hometown, we immediately went to the hospital. Mother roused slightly but was under heavy sedation. We stayed with her for a few minutes before going to my sister's home and planned to return to the hospital early the next morning.

Mother lived for eight hours that Monday, and I was privileged to be with her during that time. Just after Joye arrived in the afternoon, Mother stirred. It was as if she was waiting to say goodbye to Joye, who had cared for her for so long. Because of the stroke, her facial muscles were paralyzed on one side and she had not been able to smile. But as she roused, she *smiled*. Her expressive brown eyes opened wide. Then she went into the presence of her King.

Joye, Lynn, Tim, and I joined hands and prayed. We thanked God for a wonderful mother who demonstrated Christ to us. We rejoiced through our tears that she was home with Jesus—and with her husband, whom she loved so dearly.

And I, too, was able to say goodbye. I wouldn't have missed that for the world—certainly not for a trip to Europe! God had said no so that He could be gracious to me. His timing couldn't have been more perfect. Jack, because of plane schedules, was able to make it back for only the last part of the time at the funeral home and for the funeral itself. If I had been with him, I would have missed so much.

⑥

Our times are in God's hands. I see this all around me—in my life, in friends' lives, and in God's Word. When I first read it, I couldn't understand why the Holy Spirit chose to include the story of the Shunammite woman's house and land in the Old Testament. It appears to be such a simple story. Or is it?

Elisha had healed the son of a Shunammite woman (we don't even know her name!) and had befriended her through the years (see 2 Kings 4:8-37). One day he persuaded her to take her family and leave the country because there would be a famine for seven years (2 Kings 8:1). Upon her return, someone else had taken possession of her home and land. The "finders-keepers" rule must have applied back then. So she went to the king to appeal for her property (2 Kings 8:3-6).

Now, can you imagine the influence a Shunammite woman would have had with a king? Probably none at all.

But in God's timing, at the exact moment she entered the palace, Elisha's servant was waxing eloquent to the king concerning his master's miracles—including the one in which he had raised from death the Shunammite woman's son. Looking up, the servant exclaimed, "Oh, here she comes now!" The king asked her to tell him about it herself. Obviously impressed, he restored not only her home and land, but also the proceeds from her crops during the seven years she had been out of the country! Her visit couldn't have been timed any better!

God is not limited by time. He sees the end from the beginning. A day to Him is as a thousand years. Yet even in our human time frame He acts with accuracy.

As we search for knowledge of God, we do it primarily in two ways. First and foremost, we seek Him in His Word. When I read of His amazing timing in the details of a Shunammite woman, I marvel at God's love, His interest, and His astonishing precision.

Second, we see the knowledge and wisdom of God as He operates in our lives and in the lives of those around us. As I heard of my friends' experience in Brazil, I could not fail to worship the God who cares that much!

Jeremiah wrote, "This is what the LORD says: 'Let not the wise man boast of his wisdom or the strong man boast of his strength or the rich man boast of his riches, but let him who boasts boast about this: that he understands and knows me, that I am the LORD, who exercises kindness, justice and righteousness on earth, for in these I delight,' declares the LORD" (Jeremiah 9:23-24).

To know God. The haze in my search to understand wisdom was beginning to clear.

### FOR REFLECTION

1. When have you experienced God's perfect timing?
2. How does it make you feel to know that God cares about the smallest details of your life?

# Obtaining Wisdom

Help Lord . . .
Help Lord . . .
Help Lord . . .

A king-sized bed is far too big when you're all alone!

Jack was overseas, and I was lonely. I tossed and turned, trying to sleep. The house was too quiet. Even the wind was still. I tried praying, quoting Scripture, and thinking of clouds drifting, but sleep eluded me.

The forlorn emptiness of the bed's white expanse forced me to sit up and turn on the light. I had just been reading a book that suggested reading five Psalms each night, starting with the one numbered the same as the day of the month, and choosing the other four by adding 30, 60, 90, or 120 to the date. There are 150 Psalms, so a thirty-day month completes the book. The author suggested this would be a good thing to do before going to sleep in order to meditate on the Psalms subconsciously while sleeping. I took that to mean it might put me to sleep! I thought I would try it.

To say it failed to help me sleep would be an understatement. In fact, I got so excited about the wondrous things God showed me, I had a hard time sleeping all night! But it was worth every minute of wakefulness.

It was the sixth day of October, so I read Psalm 6 without finding anything special for my situation. When I read Psalm 36 next, however, I sat straight up in bed. I read, "They drink their fill of the abundance of Thy house; and Thou dost give them to drink of the river of Thy delights" (36:8, NASB).

God put this picture into my mind: He was sitting on His throne, and from His throne was flowing a great, wide, deep, sparkling river—the river of His delights. He was smiling and inviting me to drink.

I was standing on the bank of this wonderful river of delights, getting very thirsty. So I finally reached into my pocket and got out a little demitasse spoon, dipped it into the river, and took a sip. After a while I became thirsty again, so once more I took a spoonful from the river.

God smiled as He said, "Carole, why don't you really *drink*? Look down beside you. There is a great big ten-gallon container. Pick it up and drink fully—or better yet, why don't you just jump right in My river and let it flow all over you?"

I knew what He was saying. Sometimes I am content with so *little* when He wants to give me so *much*! But in my heart, I want to drink *deeply*, fully, and freely of His river of delights. And He *wants* me to drink. However, I often dip in with only a demitasse spoon.

"Lord," I prayed, "give me an insatiable thirst for Your delights, a hunger for Your righteousness, and a continual desire to have more of You."

God is the Source. He is the source of delight and the source of wisdom. Only as we have Him will we be wise and fulfilled.

What I had suspected all along was confirmed now in my mind. Wisdom starts with God and continues as we experience God in Christ. I read, "It is because of him that you are in Christ Jesus, who has *become* for us *wisdom* from God—that is, our righteousness, holiness and redemption" (1 Corinthians 1:30, emphasis added).

My longing to be a wise and understanding person, therefore, begins and ends with God Himself. I accept that, but how do I take it from "up there" into the "down here" in my life?

As I continued in Psalm 36, I read, "For with you is the fountain of life; in your light we see light" (36:9).

It came to me then! It is only by the Holy Spirit's illuminating power that I comprehend the light (or truths) from the Word of

God. I can "turn off" that light by blocking the Spirit or keeping the Book closed. God won't force His wisdom on me or force me to use what He has already given. I must open my mind to Him by memorizing and meditating on Scripture; I must open my heart to Him by praying; I must open my life to Him by spending time in His Word and letting His Word dwell in me. If I keep that light turned *on*, His wisdom will begin to flow into and operate in my life.

It's frightening to me to realize that the wisest king of all became a foolish man at one point in his life. God gave wisdom to Solomon, a wisdom that was accepted and used, resulting in prosperity, riches, and peace. Still, Solomon turned off the light! He disobeyed God by marrying heathen women who led him to build temples to their gods. Eventually this led Solomon away from God. "Solomon was no longer interested in the Lord God of Israel who had appeared to him twice to warn him specifically against worshiping other gods. But he hadn't *listened*" (1 Kings 11:10, TLB, emphasis added).

King Solomon didn't *hear*.

One key character trait for a wise person is that she *hears*.

It looks simple when written that way, doesn't it? Oh that it were! There are a great many octopus-like arms to that statement, and those tentacles reach everywhere. A truly wise person doesn't filter out what she doesn't wish to hear or filter in only what she wants to hear. She hears *explicitly* what is communicated—both by God and by people.

Now, none of us is perfectly wise, and often we become subjective listeners. We pick up on a certain word, tone of voice, or facial expression and balloon its importance out of all proportion. A wise person will be alert to this danger and determine to ask enough questions to clarify an unclear meaning.

A while ago, I talked with a young wife at a conference. She was downcast as she said, "This has been a wonderful conference, but instead of being encouraged I am feeling utterly defeated. At the tea, when the guest speaker shared, I thought, 'I want to be like her, but I never will be. How can I ever hope to be the godly woman that she is?' I feel like giving up and not even trying."

The guest speaker was a friend of mine. In her message she had shared her life in an open, honest way—her defeats and failures, as well as her victories. She stated that although she had lost many skirmishes, she knew Christ would win the war. She had readily admitted her shortcomings, but my young companion had not *believed* her. She had not really heard with her heart all that the speaker was saying. At that time, she had become a selective hearer, picking up only a part of what was said and magnifying that part.

There are reasons for our selective listening. One of the foremost reasons is that we hear with *limited knowledge*. I am aware that in many situations I hear only partially. And frankly, this scares me. For in hearing only part of what's being said, I can hear and interpret 100 percent *wrong*.

A second reason for selective listening is that we hear from a *limited viewpoint*. We continually filter information through our own experiences, personality, and background. My personality is very subjective, so when I hear a friend's heartbreaking tale of a cruel husband, I become so emotionally involved that it may be difficult for me to see the husband's side at all. My viewpoint is controlled by my love for my friend and my subjective nature.

A third reason for hearing selectively is that we listen with *a closed mind*—the "I've made up my mind, don't confuse me with the facts" attitude. In my own eyes, I'm right. Yet Solomon warned us that "the way of a fool seems right to him, but a wise man listens to advice" (Proverbs 12:15).

Wisdom is the ability to hear *without filtering* what is unpleasant or disagreeable. Wisdom comes from being wide open to hear God. "Ears that hear and eyes that see—the LORD has made them both" (Proverbs 20:12).

Though we must first listen to God, true wisdom is also quick to hear others. "Listen to counsel and accept discipline, that you may be wise the rest of your days" (Proverbs 19:20, NASB) and "Pay attention and listen to the sayings of the wise" (Proverbs 22:17) are verses that constantly challenge me.

My wisest counselor is Jack. And yet, because I love him so much, it's hard to take correction from him because it's impossible to be objective about things he suggests. He's aware of this and is extra careful and loving when he tells me something I need to hear. But he does tell me! Proverbs 27:6 (NASB) says, "Faithful are the wounds of a friend"—and Jack and I are best friends.

I must admit I shy away from reproof. I squint between

half-closed eyes, hoping to block out most of what someone thinks is wrong with me. But God doesn't let me get away with it for long. His Word thunders to my heart, "Do not reprove a scoffer, lest he hate you. Reprove a wise man, and he will love you. Give instruction to a wise man, and he will be still wiser. Teach a righteous man, and he will increase his learning" (Proverbs 9:8-9, NASB).

Now, I can just hear someone saying, "But surely some people who reprove you are wrong. Why, sometimes even Jack must be wrong. Are all reproofs to be taken at face value?"

No. (Aren't you relieved?)

How do you sort them out?

Jack and I have often discussed how blind spots can develop in our lives, resulting in the possibility of getting off course just one degree now and ending up ninety degrees off ten years from now. We've also talked about how to prevent this from happening. We've concluded that if anyone reproves us about anything, the first thing is to take it to the Lord, thank Him for it, and let Him search our hearts to see if part or all of the criticism is true. If God confirms it, we ask Him to change it in our lives; if not, we ask Him to help us forget it and forgive the one who has unjustly accused us. The truth is, we don't have an option about doing this because 1 Peter 2:20-21 says, "For what credit is there if, when you sin and are harshly treated, you endure it with patience? But if when you do what is right and suffer for it you patiently endure it, this finds favor with God. For you have been called for this purpose, since Christ also suffered for you, leaving you an example for you to follow in His steps" (NASB). Rather potent, isn't it?

This was a tough passage for me! I could appreciate the fact that I should patiently accept criticism that was *true*, but to accept every unjust criticism *patiently*? Whew!

But God showed me why: Any sensible person can accept with patience what is true. To accept what is untrue with love and forgiveness takes *wisdom*. Further, to be able to accept unjust criticism with the right attitude requires that *God* is the sufficient One in my life.

If two people come to Jack and me about the same thing, the process is the same, except we do even more research and praying about the matter. We know we had better take a good look at ourselves in the light of how people are seeing us because we are responsible for the *impressions* we give, even if our motives are not at fault.

Jack and I have concluded that one way to avoid the blind spots we fear is really to listen to people and listen to God Himself. He says, "Turn to my reproof, behold, I will pour out my spirit on you; I will make my words known to you" (Proverbs 1:23, NASB).

Isn't that great? We have God's promise that He will make His counsel known to us. He will give us wisdom as we truly listen.

We have God's word on it! And it is sufficient.

> *Lord, open my ears! So much of what I read in Your Word speaks of the importance of hearing. Wisdom demands it; righteousness requires it; understanding necessitates it. I see so much selective hearing. Am I a selective listener? Do I only hear what I want to? Oh, Father! You know I long to be wise, understanding, and discerning. Teach me to listen to people, experiences, expressions, tones of voice—and to life itself—with an openness of mind, a totality of heart, and an abandonment of my own preconceived ideas. Help me to learn. Teach me to open my ears and really hear. Thank You. Amen.*

## FOR REFLECTION

1. Do you drink your fill of God's delight, or do you stand at the edge of the river and sip a spoonful at a time? How can you "dive into" God's delights?

2. How good are you at hearing? What can you do to listen more closely to those around you? To God?

# CHAPTER FOUR

# Godly Wisdom

Help Lord . . .
Help Lord . . .
Help Lord . . .

Who comes to mind when you think of wisdom? How do you measure their wisdom? In his epistle, James asks the same question and gives us a complete—if seemingly impossible—answer.

> Who among you is wise and understanding? Let him show by his good behavior his deeds in the gentleness of wisdom. But if you have bitter jealousy and selfish ambition in your heart, do not be arrogant and so lie against the truth. . . . The wisdom from above is first pure, then peaceable, gentle, reasonable, full of mercy and good fruits, unwavering, without hypocrisy. And the seed whose fruit is righteousness is sown in peace by those who make peace. (James 3:13-14,17-18, NASB)

### Wisdom from Above Is Pure

I tried to act nonchalant, as if this were an everyday occurrence. But inside, way down deep where no one can see, I was jumping up and down, exclaiming, "Whoopee! Isn't this something!"

Jack and I were in Washington, D.C., and had the privilege of dining with an old friend who was serving in the U.S. Senate. His schedule was tight because the Senate was in session, so he elected to take us to the Senate dining room for lunch.

We walked down a long corridor, rode a "senators only" compartment on the tram between buildings, went up in a "senators only" elevator, and then were ushered into the senators' dining room.

I hadn't yet overcome my awe when a petite, pretty woman darted over to our friend and started talking with him. He introduced us to her, and as I was shaking her hand my mind slowly grasped whom I was meeting—Ann Landers!

So there we were, in the prestigious Senate dining room with Ann Landers and a famous senator at a table immediately behind us, talking with one of the outstanding Christian congressmen of our country. Yes, I was impressed!

Then we were served our food by a smiling waitress. Our host didn't need to tell us that the waitress was a sister in Christ—it was evident from her radiant face—but he told us something of her life and how she lived for Christ.

As we sat there eating a delicious lunch, I thought, *From a human viewpoint, this is a very prestigious group. One would be hard put to decide who is the wisest person here. But I wonder how God sees us?*

James described godly wisdom as, first of all, *pure*. Why is it that? I think James must have started with this characteristic because in this passage he also describes natural wisdom. He tells us that our natural wisdom is characterized by selfish ambition and bitter jealousy.

In contrast, God's wisdom has a completely different attitude. Godly wisdom isn't interested in looking out for "number one." It does not get jealous when someone else you know has more success than you do.

The higher your position, the more you have to guard against jealousy and selfish ambition. God is not impressed by fame, prestige, or intellectual prowess. He looks for purity of heart. I couldn't help but wonder, that afternoon in the Senate dining room, if our waitress would overshadow all the others—in God's sight—for having a wisdom that is "first of all, pure."

## Wisdom from Above Is Peaceable

My mother had a heart for the teenagers in our small Michigan town. As my brother and I began high school, she organized and led a Bible study for teens. Attendance grew in number to about thirty enthusiastic young people.

During that time, Mother developed a tumor that required surgery. She was determined that even while recuperating she would continue with the Bible study group. She would remain in bed until the group assembled at our home, then put on a hostess gown and come downstairs to teach us. The gown she most frequently wore was one of my favorites. It was white silky material with roses imprinted in a cascade down one side.

For some reason unknown to us, one woman in our town had a hate campaign going against Mother and spread vicious rumors about her. The story she made up at this time was that Mother was trying to impress the teenagers by dramatically sweeping downstairs for an "entrance" in a white gown with a sheaf of roses on her arm!

I was furious. I wanted to tell that woman how untrue and unkind her remarks were — and tell her forcefully!

The situation must have concerned Mother as well. But she did something I have never forgotten. She arranged with a local florist to send this woman one red rose every day for a week. Attached to the rose was a card with a verse of Scripture and a note of encouragement.

God used those guileless messages of love and forgiveness to break down a wall of hate. The woman didn't say anything at the time, if I recall correctly, but later on became one of Mother's staunchest supporters.

Wisdom is peaceable. It makes peace. It wins peace.

## Wisdom from Above Is Gentle

Like purity and peace, gentleness is a fruit of the Spirit as well as a characteristic of wisdom. (I equate purity with "goodness" in Galatians 5:22-23, where the fruit of the Spirit are listed.) And it certainly takes the Holy Spirit in my life to make me gentle!

One night, I was mentally making a difficult phone call concerning a frustrating situation. I projected my imagination in a dozen different versions of "He said . . ." then "I said. . . ." I was getting angrier all the time, lying there in the darkness, as sleep evaded me. (After all, how could I go to sleep in the middle of an argument, even an imaginary one?)

Finally, at 1:30 A.M. I gave up trying and tiptoed into another room to pick up my Bible. Colossians 3:13-14 grabbed me by the scruff of my argument and shook my anger with a vengeance! "Be gentle and ready to forgive; never hold grudges. Remember, the Lord forgave you, so you must forgive others. Most of all, let love guide your life, for then the whole church will stay together in perfect harmony" (TLB).

I made that phone call the next day after asking God to make me wise with His love and gentleness and to erase all my "vain imaginings." God brought a solution to my frustrations and a peaceful outcome to the problem. His wisdom covered everything.

In myself I have no wisdom, and it doesn't seem like I'm getting more as time goes on! The only thing that is changing is that I'm letting God utilize His wisdom more effectively in my life. I still ignore Him at times, but my constant prayer is, "Lord, help me to know You, to be filled full with You, so that I will walk in wisdom. I know and believe that You are all-wise."

Colossians 3:16 speaks clearly, "Remember what Christ taught and let his words enrich your lives and make you wise" (TLB).

### Wisdom from Above Is Reasonable

I grew up with one brother, one sister, and a father who was a full-blooded Dutchman. The combination led to great and glorious arguments. We argued when we knew we were wrong. We relished taking the opposite viewpoint on any topic for the sheer delight of the fray. There was no such thing as "giving in." If we were getting verbally mutilated, we simply shouted louder or walked away. To reason quietly, to compromise, or to conclude an argument never entered our thinking.

Then I married Jack. He is logical and reasonable. Seldom could I entice him into a good argument unless he knew it was important and he was correct. How irritating!

But Jack has taught me a great deal about the reasonableness of wisdom, a characteristic which, as *The Living Bible* says, "is willing to yield to others" (James 3:17, TLB). Willing to *yield*? Whoever heard of doing that?

One of the most helpful things Jack and I have learned is the use of "feedback" in communication. This is especially helpful in discussing conflicting ideas. When Jack states his point of view, I say, "If I am hearing you correctly, this is what you are saying . . ." and I repeat what I think he means. He has the opportunity to agree or to correct my restatement. He does the same with my opinions. We've found this to be a real asset in clarifying our true understanding of each other. It also helps me to see a situation from his point of view rather than only from my own. In doing this, we are both willing to yield, to compromise, or to "agree to disagree" for a time. I'm learning that wisdom is reasonable. It really does bear up under scrutiny.

### Wisdom from Above Is Full of Mercy and Good Fruits

Throughout the New Testament we find Christ, who is wisdom, showing abundant mercy and doing good to people. Now that I am a mother-in-law, I have taken special note of Peter's concern for his mother-in-law when she was running a high fever (Mark 1:29-31). Finding her ill, Peter, along with his brother and James and John, quickly told Jesus, who immediately did something about the situation. He went to her, took her hand, and healed her. Scripture tells us she then got up and began to serve them.

As I pondered this incident, it occurred to me that we often try to reverse the process. Peter's mother-in-law was touched by Christ, healed, and *then* she served them. We try to serve Him before we have been touched by Him—before He has healed us. It seems that we try to heal ourselves by working for Him, instead of waiting for His healing and then serving out of love and gratitude. And we wonder why we aren't more effective in our service!

But Christ understands our frailties and how we sometimes get things backwards. He is always full of mercy, and His mercy is evident in the way He continually ministers to us.

### Wisdom from Above Does What Is Right

A variety of words are used in different Bible versions for the next attribute of wisdom: "unwavering" (NASB); "without partiality" (KJV); "without uncertainty" (RSV); and "straightforward" (PH). It means that a wise person would follow the right course of action no matter who was involved, and would be resolute in doing it, knowing that it was right. It means hanging on to a decision no matter what adverse winds might blow and whatever the consequences.

The best piece of advice I ever heard a mother give was offered by a woman in my hometown who had three very active boys— the best behaved boys around. When asked the secret of her success, she said, "I never say no unless I have to. But when I have to, I never make an exception. I mean it." She was an unusual mother, and one whose wisdom was unwavering.

### Wisdom from Above Is Without Hypocrisy

Who comes immediately to mind when you think of the quality of being without hypocrisy? Who would you name as a sincere, guileless person? To me, Lorne Sanny, a former president of The Navigators, is one who epitomizes this characteristic.

When Jack and I first joined the staff of The Navigators, we lived in a small log cabin just outside the gates of Glen Eyrie, headquarters for The Navigators in Colorado Springs. Jack helped with conferences and managed the print shop, a job he really didn't know much about. Jack also had the privilege of working closely with Lorne.

Lorne's attitude toward me has been exactly the same throughout the years—gracious, kind, and friendly. To me, he is the embodiment of a sincere man, without a shred of hypocrisy in his makeup, and I appreciate this quality in him.

In the light of these qualities of godly wisdom, is it any wonder that James asked the searching question, "Who among you is wise and understanding?" (James 3:13, NASB). His subsequent statement is profound: "Let him show [demonstrate] by his good behavior his deeds in the gentleness of wisdom." The qualities of wisdom are not in words but in actions. They are seen in our behavior and our deeds, and the sum of them is "the gentleness of wisdom."

### Day-to-Day Wisdom

It was a sparkling day in Colorado. As I drove toward the mountains, I thought, *Lord, I can't even imagine heaven being more beautiful than this. What a Creator You are!*

On my way home from running my errand, again I observed God's handiwork and thought how wonderful it would be to go Home . . . to be with God in a twinkling. I said, "Lord, I'd just like to go Home right now. I guess lots of people long for heaven when things are really bad, but somehow right now, in the beauty of this moment, I long to go to heaven just so I can see more of You, and get to know You better."

Within my heart, God answered with a thought I'd never considered before. He said, "Carole, you are getting to know Me on earth in ways that will be impossible in Heaven."

As I pondered this, I suddenly realized what He was saying. We get to know God through suffering here. There will be no suffering in heaven. We learn how to see God through tears, feel His comfort in pain, and hear His voice of strength in trials and tribulations. There will be no tears, no pain, no trials, no tribulation in heaven. So in unique and precious ways, we get to know God differently down here. We are learning things about Him we could *never* discover in heaven! And we can take that knowledge with us when we go to be with Him forever.

No wonder we are to welcome trials as *friends*. No wonder we are to count it all *joy* to suffer!

I'm sure God smiled when, after getting really excited about this wonderful truth, I had to tell Him, "That's exciting, Father. But I still don't think I'll ask for more pain, if You don't mind. I want to get to know You more than, well, most anything . . . but I'm still a coward. Still, send me what You know is best for me."

I know He will.

I believe God gave me a bit of wisdom that day—insight into His plan and purpose for the pain in my life. Glimpses of truth from God can be one way to gauge whether we are open to His wisdom. Is He teaching us new and precious truths about Himself each day, each week? God is such a many-splendored Person that we will never come to the end of learning fresh lessons about His character. If we aren't learning about Him, it isn't God's fault. It's ours for not opening ourselves to His teaching.

I began to think about other tangible signs of God's wisdom in our lives and realized that we find some measuring sticks in the Bible that help us know whether we are being open to Him.

These measuring sticks can take the form of asking ourselves such questions as, "Who am I close to?" "Who influences me?" "What voice or voices am I taking careful note of?" When Jack and I asked a member of Congress what kind of leader a newly elected president would make, his wise reply was, "I'm waiting to find out what kind of men he will gather around him." Solomon, the wisest king of all history, declared, "A wise man will hear and increase in learning, and a man of understanding will acquire wise counsel" (Proverbs 1:5, NASB).

Not only will a wise person seek qualified counselors, she will also carefully select her friends and companions. God warns us that "he who walks with the wise grows wise, but a companion of fools suffers harm" (Proverbs 13:20).

In a great many instances we allow ourselves to be influenced wrongly. Often, very subtly and without thinking, we listen to the clamoring voices around us and buy whatever philosophy the world is selling today. Our minds are deluged with a flood of worldly ideas, and we may drown without a struggle, not realizing we've been easy victims.

One concept we have bought from the world concerns expressing our anger. We're told that it is not healthy to repress our emotions, that we must let them all hang out. But Scripture tells us we are to be slow to anger, to be cool in our spirits, to think before we speak. We *do* have to get it out, but we can get it out to God and let Him handle our feelings, erase our anger, or help us manage that anger with wisdom that is pure and gentle.

Our standards of purity are also subjected to a not-so-quiet brainwashing process by television, books, movies, magazines, and newspapers. But we are warned, "Don't let the world around you squeeze you into its own mold" (Romans 12:2, PH).

One of the ways to combat these kinds of pressures from the world is to ask God to surround us with wise people as our counselors, friends, and companions—individuals who will sharpen us, challenge us, and instruct us. They should be friends whose eyes are on the Lord and who will help us keep our eyes on Him too.

Another way to stand strong against the world is to lead a life marked by discipline and obedience. "Whoso keepeth the law is a wise son" (Proverbs 28:7, KJV). Jesus said, "Therefore everyone who hears these words of mine and puts them into practice is like a wise man who built his house on the rock" (Matthew 7:24).

The behavior of a wise person will demonstrate understanding. It will be good behavior. A wise person won't lie or be lazy. She won't say that wrong is right or show partiality. Her tongue will bring healing and will make knowledge acceptable. She will learn by observation.[1]

How amazing are wisdom's results! In Proverbs 24:13-14 we are told that wisdom is sweet like honey to the soul. "If you find it, then there will be a future, and your hope will not be cut off" (NASB).

I realize that only a fraction of the tip of an iceberg shows as I write these chapters and learn more about wisdom. God's wisdom—the kind He wants to give me—is a concept I trust will be growing in me for the rest of my life.

But the twofold aspect of my first feeble prayer is crystal clear now. The request in the first part of Psalm 90:12—"Teach us to number our days"—puts the responsibility squarely on God to teach me as I ask Him. It is His promise to train me in wisdom. The second part of the verse, "that we may present to Thee a heart of wisdom," pointedly shows me my duty to listen, to be open to His light, to search my heart, and then to present, or, as the King James Version translates, to "apply" my heart to wisdom. With these shining truths radiating around me, I look to heaven and say, "Thank You, Father. What next?"

## FOR REFLECTION

1. Think about the characteristics of wisdom in this chapter. In which areas do you need some development?

2. Find a verse that describes one of the characteristics of wisdom. Memorize it and pray over it, asking God to apply that area of wisdom to your life.

# CHAPTER FIVE

# Wisdom in Marriage

Help Lord . . .
Help Lord . . .
Help Lord . . .

To be a wife is an adventure! One day as I was contemplating this concept, I began to see how much wisdom I needed for my adventure-vocation. A verse rang an alarm in my mind: "The wise woman builds her house, but with her own hands the foolish one tears hers down" (Proverbs 14:1). God had begun to give me a glimpse of what wisdom was, and now He was telling me what to do with it. I was to build my house. But what was my "house"? I concluded that a woman's house consisted of the people in her sphere of influence.

Every woman builds or tears down. No neutral ground is possible. In my mind I paraphrased that verse, "A wise woman builds into the lives of those around her, but a foolish woman tears down others' lives." This brought my thinking to the one closest to me — my husband. I was to build up my husband, not tear him down. And this building was a many-faceted task.

I often ask this question of women who are contemplating marriage: "Is God calling you to be this man's wife?" Marriage should not be something one drifts into or decides to do in order to get out of something else. It should be a call from God — as important a calling as a call to the mission field or a call to full-time Christian service. And it is a unique call.

The last part of Romans 8:28 tells us that we are called according to God's purpose. God leads us in the way we should go, and He will guide us with His counsel.[1] His holy calling for us is "not according to our works, but according to His own purpose and grace which was granted us in Christ Jesus from all eternity" (2 Timothy 1:9, NASB). Therefore, if He has led us and guided us to be married, we are called to that specific plan of His for our lives.

If we realize deep within our hearts that marriage is a call from God, our attitudes change. If we view marriage as just another job and just another situation, we begin to complain when things get rough, and some even start to think of ways to get out.

If we knew beyond all doubt that we had received a call to the mission field and then began to experience persecution or saw few results for our labors, we would still believe it was God's overall plan for us. We would try not to doubt what God had called us to do.

Something of the same is true in our marriages. When we know that it is God's call for us to be a wife, our perspective alters. When things become difficult, we can believe it is part of God's plan to perfect us, to help us know Him, to strengthen us to work through the difficulties, and to be fruitful for Him.

When you are assured that God's call for you is to be a wife, you can begin with assurance to discover what that ministry includes. You can ask a creative God for creative ideas to develop your ministry and so build into the life of your husband.

### Growing with Him

Raindrops splattered on our windshield. Except for the accompanying purr of the engine, they provided the only sound in our car. I was thinking of the conversation Jack had just related.

During a recent five-hour flight across the United States, Jack asked his seat companion, "Why are you moving to California?"

"A good marriage gone bad," the young woman said, as her wry smile refused to reach her eyes.

She poured out a familiar story to Jack's sympathetic ear. She had worked to put her husband through law school. Now that he was a successful lawyer, he had met someone else. According to the young wife, the other woman wasn't physically attractive, but the husband was divorcing her to marry the woman for intellectual reasons.

I reflected then on the importance of a wife *growing* with her husband.

In graduate school, Jack and I lived in a twenty-eight-foot trailer parked in "Trailerville," with about forty others, on the school grounds. Because we didn't have children in our school days, our trailer was often the gathering place for some of the men to discuss deep theological and philosophical issues. Even when I went to bed before their conversations ended, I could hear them through the thin door separating the bedroom from the living room. I listened whether I wanted to or not!

As the years have gone by, I've made it my goal to learn about the things that interest Jack. It's our responsibility as wives to grow and learn alongside our husbands so that we can discuss ideas and debate issues.

### Knowing Him

Often we hear about how important it is to study the man God has given to us, but no one tells us how! In order to build into the lives of our husbands, we have to know them. And knowing them, truly knowing them, will take years of study. They are constantly changing, as we are, so this task will never be finished. But what satisfying work, with lasting rewards! God will give us understanding to ensure success.

One of the first things to learn in order to study your husband is the art of asking questions that are interesting for him to answer, informative to you, deep in quality, and nonthreatening. Let me offer you seven questions as a test to see how well you know your husband. (You might want to use these same questions on "dates" with your husband as a springboard for some interesting conversations.)

1. What is the happiest thing that has ever happened to your husband?
2. What has been the hardest experience of his life?
3. What are his secret ambitions, his life goals?
4. What are his deepest fears?
5. What does he most appreciate about you?
6. What traits of yours would he like to see changed?
7. What man or men does he most admire?

One way to come up with interesting questions that will stim- ulate conversation is to make notes and write down thoughts or questions whenever you read a book. You might ask other wives for good questions, or take a course in family counseling, or read a book on counseling to gather ideas on ways to keep communi- cation flowing or break through the barrier of silence that sometimes builds up.

Pray, asking our inventive God for ideas to build bridges of communication. Ask your husband for his schedule as the day begins—his appointments, meetings, and important decisions that need to be made. As you pray through your day, pray through his as well. You will find yourself more involved in your husband's life and able to ask him knowledgeable questions.

Second, study his habits and his work. Is he a prompt person, or is he habitually late? Is he a morning, afternoon, or evening per- son? Neat or casual? Does he dream at night? Daydream? Fantasize? If so, what about? Is he disciplined? In what areas? What bores him about his work, stimulates him, or disturbs him?

Ask yourself a hundred questions, and then study him to find the answers. Know him. Find out what makes him angry, bored, slightly irritated, amused, or discouraged. Study him!

### Appreciating Him

The Bible says, "Do not withhold good from those who deserve it, when it is in your power to act" (Proverbs 3:27). As I was think- ing about this verse, I realized it is a command from God. So when I fail to obey it, it is sin. Did you ever think it sin to fail to encour- age or appreciate someone? Because God commands it, He will give us the ability and many "nudgings" to speak up when we like something and not withhold that good word.

At times we must ask God for an awareness to speak a word of appreciation. We take so much for granted, don't we? (And then we complain because our husbands seem to take us for granted!) Have you thanked your husband lately for working long hours for you and the children? For coming home on time or calling you when he couldn't? For changing the oil in the car? For keeping the grass cut and shoveling the walks? Have you told him you're glad he chose you to marry and that you appreciate his concern when you don't feel well?

Have you complimented him recently on those qualities you first fell in love with — his strength, his sense of humor, his brown eyes? Perhaps I haven't hit one thing that's true about your husband. But think hard, my friend, and pray much concerning ways in which you can appreciate your husband and show him you adore him.

One of the most effective ways to build into the life of your husband and let him know you appreciate him is by constantly assuring him you are 100 percent with him. I remember vividly a time when I completely failed Jack in this.

It had been a period of utter frustration for me. We were in a Navigator home, with four men living with us for training in Christian discipleship and to help lead our ministry. The work involved was staggering. But that wasn't my frustration, for I thrived on such responsibilities.

It was Jack. For several weeks he had been extremely distant, moody, and noncommunicative. Every time I tried to break through the wall of indifference (that was what it seemed like to me), the barrier seemed to get thicker. Even my withdrawal into a silence of my own (which is so unusual that he almost always has to respond) went unnoticed. I began to feel like a part of the furniture or, at best, a hired hand without pay, instead of a wife and companion. My attitude got worse. But he seemingly didn't notice.

Finally, I erupted! I walked into his study and let him have it — *pow!*—right between the eyes in a verbal blast. I told him I was leaving for the day (Lynn was at school), that I didn't know what time I would be back, and I didn't know where I was going and didn't care, for I couldn't stand it any longer.

He did look at me then — really looked at me. I will never forget the wounded expression in his eyes as he said slowly, "Are you against me *too*?"

I had blasted the wall away all right, and all his bruised and infected wounds were revealed. He was undergoing severe criticism from some of those who were living in our home. He had been left stabbed and bleeding, and he had wanted to spare me from knowing his hurt. So he was trying to bear the pain all by himself, and in so doing had caused me to be "against" him too. I had completely misinterpreted the reason for his mood.

We wept together.

We agreed we would never again hide things from each other and never try to endure injuries alone.

But what a lesson for this wife! At a time when Jack needed my confidence, my support, my help, I had let him down because I was not, at that time, 100 percent with him. It is a lesson I will never forget.

### Enjoying Him

Do you really enjoy your husband? I'm not just talking about sex. Do you enjoy simply being with him—running errands, grocery shopping, sitting around on a Sunday afternoon with the newspaper?

As a result of a "marital intimacy" test some time ago, Jack and I discovered that we rated lowest on "recreational intimacy." He has always been athletic, but that's not one of my strong suits (the understatement of the year!).

As we talked about it, we decided to take up tennis together, a game I learned to love. I also determined that after twenty-five years of being a spectator, I would take up golf. Jack loves to play golf, and our vacations usually include someplace where there is a beautiful course. While I have always enjoyed driving the cart for him, it isn't always possible on crowded courses. I've had to pray for two things: a genuine liking for golf (I knew I'd never really pursue it if I didn't like it) and enough ability not to feel like an utter fool. God has given me the first; the second I'm still praying for! It may have me licked, but even if I sell my clubs, the fact that I've taken some golf lessons and played for many summers has given me a much greater appreciation of Jack's skill, and I will have even more fun driving his cart while on vacation.

⑥

The name of the game is change. And it's a game we can win as we claim the promise of Philippians 4:13: "I can do everything through him who gives me strength."

When was the last time your husband, or someone else, made a suggestion to you, and you said (or thought), "But that's just the way I am?" When was the last time God showed you something you should alter? If He doesn't do it frequently, you've stopped listening!

What's on your prayer list concerning changes that need to take place in your life and personality, your husband's life and personality, and your children's lives? What's on your prayer list concerning interests you as a couple can share? Are you praying that you will have more fun together? That you will be better friends? That you will enjoy one another increasingly?

Remember, my friend, what Scripture says:

> Two are better than one because they have a good return for their labor. For if either of them falls, the one will lift up his companion. But woe to the one who falls when there is not another to *lift him up*. (Ecclesiastes 4:9-10, NASB, emphasis added)

> *Lord, what a beautiful picture of marriage! Not two halves of a couple, but two people being and doing more together than they could have been or done alone. Not just double effectiveness, but multiplied effectiveness! An integral part of marriage is being all I was meant to be as a person, and even more! Thank You for giving me a partner who makes me know this is true. Amen.*

### FOR REFLECTION

1. How would your attitude toward your marriage change if you viewed it as a call from God?
2. What are some ways you could grow with your husband?
3. Think of some creative ways to show your husband how much you appreciate him. Keep the list handy and use an idea or two a week. Which ideas will you try this week?

CHAPTER SIX

# The Goal
# of Our Lives

Help Lord . . .
Help Lord . . .
Help Lord...

Three phone calls before 10:00 A.M. that Saturday morning suddenly turned my day gloomy. Each call was from a person who was hurting, someone I cared about very much. After the third call, I returned to my room, picked up my Bible, and opened it to the third chapter of Colossians. God began a process that morning of hammering home a lesson that He hasn't yet stopped teaching me. As I read, He spoke very forcefully to my heart from the first two verses: "Since, then, you have been raised with Christ, set your hearts on things above, where Christ is seated at the right hand of God. Set your minds on things above, not on earthly things."

As I read in His Word, God was teaching me His ways: "Carole, you must not set your mind on anything but Me. You must keep setting your mind on and continually seeking the things which are above. Do not focus your mind on people's problems. Share their burdens, yes, but don't allow your mind to be occupied with these burdens. Set your mind on Me." That day grew noticeably brighter.

There was more to learn . . . and learn, and learn.

One week after that Saturday, when a long-awaited trip overseas was canceled, God taught me another important principle.

"Carole, don't set your heart on trips on earth. Your sights aren't high enough. Set your mind on your heavenly journey. Set your mind on Me." (*All right, Lord. That, too.*)

Sudden, violent storms all through the South and Midwest caused another trip to be radically altered, and God gently reminded me, "Don't set your heart on a fixed schedule of events. I am in control. Set your heart on Me." (*Another facet? All right, Father. I think I'm getting the picture.*)

And then the day came when all these pressures and problems left me teary and shaky inside. I'm not that way very often. It frightens me when I run on the fine line of tears at any moment. That day God's persistent voice said, "Carole. One more thing. Don't set your mind on your ability or inability to be strong inside. Set your mind on Me." (*Was I finally getting it? It seemed as though it didn't matter whoever, whenever, whatever my focal point. If the focus wasn't on God, it was wrong!*)

As I read Evelyn Christenson's excellent book *Lord, Change Me!*, God spoke greatly to me through it. But I realized even there that I was focusing wrongly (my fault, not hers). I was emphasizing "Lord, change *me*" and God wanted it "*Lord*, change me!"

It took several weeks for me to read past Colossians 3:1-2 because God kept stopping me right there. As I finally got to verse 3, I almost laughed out loud. There is a reason why things, problems, and people should not upset me. *I am dead.* What can upset a dead person who is perfectly hidden? This verse says that I am "hidden with Christ in God."

The secret of being dead is in verse 4, which I hastened to read. My dead person is exchanged for the person of Christ, who is my life. I felt like shouting! An exchanged life! My dead life for His life!

This verse doesn't say that Christ is a part of our lives—an addition, a helper, or a friend. He *is* our life! Did I know that in an experiential and practical way? I admitted to Him that I needed to learn a great deal more about this particular truth. And I still do.

Part of the key goes back to verse 2, the setting of my mind and the keeping of my eyes, heart, and thoughts on the goal—on Him. Hebrews 12:2-3 puts it well. We are to be "fixing our eyes on Jesus, the author and perfecter of faith, who for the joy set before Him endured the cross, despising the shame, and has sat down at the right hand of the throne of God. For consider Him who has endured such hostility by sinners against Himself, so that you may not grow weary and lose heart" (NASB).

We are to do what our example, Christ, did on earth. He kept looking at the goal, not the going. He was seeing the prize, not the process; the treasure, not the trial; the joy, not the journey. And we must do the same!

*Consider Jesus.* The answer to all of life is in those words. The two action verbs in Colossians 3:1-2 give us the answer to our discouragement, fears, and frustrations. We are to *keep seeking* heavenly things—Christ Himself—and we are to *set* our minds on Him.

I am discovering that the battle is won or lost in my mind—or will. I *choose* to lose heart, to give up, to let my mind dwell on other things. If courage is "the mental discipline to endure," then I simply decide not to endure. But I don't want to "not endure." And so goes the battle. Only God's strength and grace will win it for me.

Therein lies the key question. How, in a real and practical way, can I keep setting my mind, keep seeking, and keep on considering Jesus? How can I determine to endure instead of faint? At the moment of decision, how can I ensure that I will make the right choice?

I searched the Scriptures, but not very far this time. Because Colossians 3 not only holds the "this is what to do," but also contains the "this is how you do it"! God always tells us, but sometimes we fail to look.

The answer is found in the command, "Let the word of Christ dwell in you richly" (Colossians 3:16). I ought to know that by now! The solution lies in my day-by-day dwelling in the Word and letting the Word dwell in me. The battle to discipline my time so that I spend time with God every day will win the war for my mind. Like a marathon runner, I will stumble at times and get distracted. Perhaps this is part of the race I cannot avoid. The difference is that I'm learning how to pick myself up and set my eyes back on the goal—on what Christ intends for me to be and what He has for me eternally.

In between what we are to do (set our minds on Him) and how

we are to do it (let the Word richly dwell in us) is what we are to be in relation to those around us. We are to be compassionate, kind, humble, gentle, patient, and forgiving, and we are to walk in love and be at peace (see Colossians 3:12-15). We should also have a continually thankful heart.

In other words, *positionally* we are dead (Colossians 3:3), hidden with Christ in God and risen with Christ. The complete truth of this in our lives will be evident when we are revealed with Christ in glory (verse 4).

We are learning to become *practically*—in practice—what we already are *positionally*! When we become new persons in Christ, we really are dead to immorality, idolatry, and the other things mentioned in verse 5. Most of us don't have a lot of trouble with those—at least not often. But we have to continually *put aside* anger, wrath, malice, slander, and abusive speech (verse 8) by an act of our wills. This is the process involved in putting on our new self and being renewed in a true knowledge of Christ (see Ephesians 4:23-24).

There are times when I get very upset with the unequal way people are treated. I can feel my fighting blood begin to boil as women are ignored, minorities are put down, or the poor are mistreated. As Christians, we should be growing in our ability to view people as God views us: that is, without distinctions (Colossians 3:11). But even this isn't going far enough. While I am to regard people without partiality or distinction, the main truth I must know is that *Christ is all, and He is in all.* Some of us get so caught up in the fight for equality that we forget to keep our eyes on the Master instead of the battle. Christ will fight for us or will lead us to take up the sword. The fight must not be our main concern, but our obedience to Him should be. If we were obedient and had hearts of compassion along with the other characteristics listed in Colossians 3:12-14, it would be automatic to make no distinction between people.

A wise woman builds into the lives of others not so much by *what* she does but by *who* she is. In the first place, it is God who does the building in people's lives. In the second place, it is only as a woman's life overflows with Him that she can bear the fruit that will last (see John 15:16). What she is dictates what she does.

I am a ministry-oriented person. I like to "do." But there have been several times in my life when the Lord has cut me off completely from what some call ministry (Bible studies, witnessing, speaking, and leading others in discipleship) in order to etch deeply in my heart that the purpose for which He created me was to know Him and to fellowship with Him.

He can get along very well without my "ministry," but how wonderful it is to know that He *longs* for my fellowship! Most of all He wants me to be with Him and to be godly, allowing the Holy Spirit full access to my life. Then He will lead me into any ministry He wants me to do and will give me the privilege of building into the lives of those around me. I cannot help others apart from knowing Him.

*Father, You know it is my desire to build up and help those around me: friends, neighbors, and others. Thank You for showing me that this building must be an overflow of Your life through me. Help me to be a clear channel for Your Spirit and to be quick to obey Your voice. Thank You. Amen.*

### FOR REFLECTION

1. On what do you set your heart? How can you learn to set it on God alone?
2. "A wise woman builds into the lives of others not so much by *what* she does but by *who* she is." How does focusing on the Father make this possible?
3. Colossians says to let the Word dwell in you richly. Are you doing this? If not, how can you make this your goal?

# CHAPTER SEVEN

# Thankfulness in Everything

Help Lord . . .
Help Lord . . .
Help Lord . . .

She was an angelic-looking little girl who had just been very bad. Sitting on her small potty-chair in the kitchen, with no one paying the slightest attention to her as we talked, she drew pictures on the wall with a dark red crayon.

Her father suddenly became aware of what she had done and said quietly, "Oh, Brenda. Daddy has told you not to draw on the walls." He lifted his tiny blond daughter off her chair, took her to the basement, and saw to it that she would remember never to do it again! Then he held her until her tears ceased and he had reassured her of his love.

Sometimes our heavenly Father's lessons hurt. But He teaches them to us justly and lovingly.

We can have no wisdom apart from being taught by God. He is a faithful, kind, and loving teacher, if we listen. In His love, He will continue to be faithful—and harder on us—if we don't listen! I pray often that I will "learn easy" because I don't like hard discipline.

God never stops teaching. I find that if He doesn't show me something new about Himself or myself each week, it isn't because He's stopped teaching, it's because I've stopped listening.

As I wrote this book, God showed me some new things about one important attitude we must have in order to build on the right foundation and be wise.

Have you noticed that when the Lord wants to get a point across, He seems to teach us in a variety of ways? Specific passages of Scripture exclaim it; people mention it; and God's reproof, correction, and instruction demand it. And then, in other Scripture, it is sort of "tucked in" as if God were saying, "Don't forget now!"

The attitude I'm talking about is stated forthrightly in 1 Thessalonians 5:18: "In everything give thanks; for this is God's will for you in Christ Jesus" (NASB). It is also one of the great truths in Philippians 4:6: "Do not be anxious about anything, but in everything, by prayer and petition, with thanksgiving, present your requests to God." It must be extremely important to God for us to be thankful because His reminders to us never cease!

There are some who wake up and cheerfully say, "Good morning, Lord." Others act like Lucy or Linus, the characters in Charles Schulz's *Peanuts*. In one cartoon, Lucy looks out the window at the pouring rain and says, "It looks like a good day." Linus answers, "What do you mean a good day? It's raining . . . it's windy . . . it's cold!" In the last frame of the cartoon Lucy answers, "It's a good day to be crabby!"

God has so much more for us than good days to be crabby! He wants us to shout within, "*This* is the day the Lord has made. Let us rejoice and be glad in it."

God is vitally interested in our outlook and our "uplook." He wants us to have a thankful spirit for our own good. If we follow His admonition to be thankful, it will make the difference between a dreary existence and an exciting life. Our lives are like mirrors that are meant to shine and clearly reflect Jesus Christ. When we let those mirrors become smudged with sin, dulled with thanklessness, and dirty with despair, not only do we fail to reflect the Son, but our own souls can't grow anything beautiful either. To some, life is a trial rather than a treasure, an adversity instead of an adventure. We are to look at life from above it because that is where we are—we are seated with Christ "in the heavenly places" (Ephesians 2:6, NASB).

And just what is a positive, thankful attitude?

The story is told of a great fire in Thomas Edison's laboratories.

Edison and his son rushed to the scene and watched while his life's work went up in flames. He turned to his son and exclaimed, "Son, go get your mother quick. She's never seen a fire like this!" The next morning the two were surveying the smoldering ruins, and Edison said, "Just think. All our mistakes have been burned up and we have a chance to start all over again." That, to me, is a positive attitude!

Most great lessons, those deeply used by God to teach us, are learned amidst the desperate events in our lives. Since the time my first book, *From the Heart of a Woman,* was published, several people have remarked to me, "I didn't realize you had such a hard life." At first I reacted to those comments with amazement. On average, I feel that God has given me a truly wonderful life in every way. Then I realized that almost every chapter of the book begins with a trial! Pushed together like that, it looks like most of my life has consisted of problems and hard circumstances. But those were my times of deepest learning, and they naturally became what I wrote about.

It was Paul's years in prison, his beatings, his painful times that gave him the authority to write about joy and to encourage others. How tragic it is when we fail to learn God's lessons because of a negative, bitter attitude.

⑥

The men trudged homeward. They numbered an even dozen, with strong swarthy faces creased by sun and desert wind. Ten of them walked with shoulders slumped, discouragement in every step—in sharp contrast to the two others who held their heads high and spring-stepped along the dusty trail.

As they returned home, a throng of people rushed to meet them and hear their report of the land that lay ahead. The ten discouraged men reported, "It's beautiful over there, but we'll never make it. The people are giants and the cities are well protected. We might as well forget it!"

But the other two, Caleb and Joshua, protested: "It is a wonderful country ahead, and the Lord loves us. He will bring us safely into the land and give it to us" (Numbers 14:7-8, TLB).

It has been said that whether life grinds a man down or polishes him depends on what he is made of. In myself, I'm not made of very stern stuff. The "me" in me wants to grumble, complain, and murmur. I am inclined to doubt, to fear, to fail. But God in me *cannot* fail. He will help me face life head-on and with joy. And I can cry with conviction, "It is a wonderful country ahead, and the Lord loves us!"

☾

It's exciting to walk with God, to let Him be the builder of our lives.

I am increasingly aware that He desires to be the architect of my total life.

If I decided to build a house, I would need an architect who could draw not only an overall plan but a detailed one. What would my house look like if, after I started building, I decided I would add another room upstairs, and later I relocated a wall, exchanged a bathroom for the utility room, and put two additional hallways somewhere? When my house was finished I would have some kind of monstrosity.

To build a house I would need both an architect and a master builder because I don't even know how to drive a nail straight. If I were to be the one to actually build this house, I would need a very patient coach who would show me how to do everything as well as help me undo any construction mistakes.

I don't know of any human architect like that. But that describes the Lord Jesus perfectly. Not only does He build our house (using our hands), but He also patiently corrects our mistakes. When we blunder by deciding to do it our way rather than His, and we're sorry for what we've done, He can even draw that horrible mistake into the plans and still have it turn out beautifully. He can make monuments out of mistakes. Given complete control, our architect—Jesus Christ—will build us a very lovely house indeed.

A house will not stand without a foundation, and we must have a very firm foundation to stand against the onslaught of the forces around us. We need Jesus Christ, not only to be our architect and builder, but to be the foundation as well. "For no one can lay any foundation other than the one already laid, which is Jesus Christ" (1 Corinthians 3:11). Life is risky and worthless without the Lord.

A commuter was overheard saying to his seat companion, "I've got a clock that tells me when to get up—but some days I need one to tell me why."

We need that sure foundation to be able to know the "why" of living. We cannot build our lives on sand; we must build on the Rock. When we receive Christ as our Savior and Lord, He is established forever as the foundation of our lives.

One of my favorite stories while growing up concerned a little boy who carved a boat with painstaking care. He sanded it and painted it a bright blue. Then he attached a long string to it and took it to a nearby creek to see if it would sail. He was thrilled that it bobbed on the water like a seagoing yacht. But suddenly a gust of wind and a stronger current caused the little boat to whirl away, and the string broke from his hand. Crestfallen, the little boy watched helplessly as his beloved boat spun from his sight around the bend where he could not follow. He thought it was gone forever.

A week later, as he was walking by a store, there in the window was his little blue boat! Joyfully he ran inside and said, "Mister, that boat in the window . . . it's mine. I made it!"

The storekeeper said, "I'm sorry, son, but I paid for that boat, and if you want it, you will have to give me one dollar to buy it."

The boy lost no time running home to shake every last penny from his piggy bank. When he discovered it wasn't enough, he knocked on the doors of neighbors, asking if he could do some work to earn more money. He finally had the dollar and ran back to the store and bought the boat. As he lovingly cradled the boat in his arms, he said, "Now you are twice mine. First I made you and then I bought you."

Exactly.

We are twice God's. First He made us, and the currents of sin and self whirled us away to become lost to Him. Then He bought us, redeeming us from the enemy of our souls with His own blood. Jesus died to buy us back for God so that we might fellowship with Him.

Unlike that little blue boat, we are given a choice of whether we want to be "bought back" by God. The price has been paid, but we can refuse to be purchased. If we say yes to His invitation, then He becomes the foundation of our lives, the author of our salvation, the builder of our eternity. If we choose to receive Him we have everything. If we choose not to receive Him we have nothing. He leaves the choice with us.

God builds into our lives in numerous ways — through His Word, through prayer, through the insights of others, through life's experiences, and in discipline. In every case, the roof over all is love.

As we "build" into peoples' lives, Scripture tells us, "Above all, keep fervent in your love for one another, because love covers a multitude of sins" (1 Peter 4:8, NASB). Love covers when friends offend us. It covers irritations, frustrations, and idiosyncrasies. And it covers both ways, doesn't it? If we really love others, we are willing and able to overlook a great many things in their lives. And if they know we love them, they are willing to overlook a great many of our faults as well. Love covers.

Let me summarize. The foundation of our house is Christ; the roof is His love; and the walls are the Word of God, prayer, obedience, fellowship with other Christians, and witnessing.

It is important to remember that as we build in others' lives, these principles of walking with God are concepts that will keep the elements of the world from destroying that house. If we lay a foundation and then fail to build the walls, we will find ourselves continually having to clear the foundation of garbage and debris. One day the wind blows leaves all over the foundation, so we work at sweeping off the leaves. The following week it snows, and we diligently shovel off the snow.

The leaves and the snow are synonymous with problems in the lives of those comprising our "house." Failing to build walls into their lives comprised of the Word and prayer will allow the winds of the world to mess up or even destroy their house.

We are all in the process of either building up or tearing down our lives and the lives of those around us. There is no possibility of maintaining status quo. A wise woman builds; a foolish woman tears down. May God grant us wisdom and teach us to number our days and apply our hearts to His wisdom so that we may present to Him a house that is a monument to His glory and useful for His service.

We have not ceased to pray for you and to ask that you may be filled with the knowledge of His will in all spiritual wisdom and understanding, so that you may walk in a manner worthy of the Lord, to please Him in all respects, bearing fruit in every good work and increasing in the knowledge of God; strengthened with all power, according to His glorious might, for the attaining of all steadfastness and patience; joyously giving thanks to the Father, who has qualified us to share in the inheritance of the saints in light. (Colossians 1:9-12, NASB)

> *Father God, how can I say "thank You" for all You have done? For opening up new truths about wisdom through Joye's illness. For teaching me that You are wisdom. You give wisdom, You build wisdom, and You are more eager for me to have it than I am eager to receive it! Thank You for showing me truths about building my house. I know it is just a beginning; please don't stop teaching. Thank You that You won't. Thank You for those around me who are "build-ing" into me . . . for Jack, Lynn, Tim, Joye, and so many friends and relatives. Thank You that they are faithful to build, even when their hammers hurt. Thank You for Your love, Your patience, Your faithfulness as You build into my life. I love You. Amen.*

### FOR REFLECTION
1. How thankful are you when things go wrong?
2. Why does God want us to be thankful in *everything*?
3. How can you step back and let Christ be the architect of your life? Would that affect your ability to be thankful? If so, how?

Help Lord . . .

Help Lord . . .

Help Lord . . .

# PART TWO
# Lord of My
# Rocking Boat

. . . I'm Sinking

# WHAT ROCKS MY BOAT?

*THE WIND CAME SUDDENLY ON THE WATER. A GIANT WAVE CAUGHT the small boat and carried it high, where it hovered for a moment on the wave's crest and then fell to the bottom of a deep trough. A succession of waves poured over the sides until the boat could only respond sluggishly as it began to fill with water.*

*The faces of the seasoned fishermen showed concern. Veterans of many storms, they instinctively knew this one spelled danger to their lives. One person aboard the boat showed no concern at all. Exhausted, He lay sleeping at one end of the small craft, oblivious to its tossing and bucking. Finally the men could stand it no longer. One touched His shoulder and shouted over the howling wind, "Teacher, don't you even care that we are all about to drown?"*

*The man opened His weary eyes slowly. His face registered many emotions—exhaustion, sadness, awareness, tenderness. Then He rose and addressed the sea. "Be quiet," He commanded.*

*Suddenly, all was still. The calm sea mirrored the sun breaking through the clouds. No whisper of wind marred the surface of the water.*

*The teacher turned to the fishermen and asked, "Why are you so fearful? Don't you have any faith?"*

At the time I read this story in Mark 4, the boat of my life was being buffeted about with many waves of circumstance and, like the disciples, I was fearful. For three years the storms had been fierce. It seemed as though when Christ spoke "Peace" to the turmoil in one area, another squall would start up somewhere else. When He calmed that one, a small hailstorm battered my boat from a different direction. I began to wonder if the sea of my life was ever going to be calm all at once!

Yet it wasn't the ferocity of the gales, it was the constancy of the minor daily struggles that kept me off balance. The ceaseless motion of those little waves—day in, day out—frequently caused me to feel uncomfortable, frustrated, and sometimes downright seasick! With one exception, it is the small but persistent trials that I want to explore with you.

How do we deal with the problems, pressures, and pains of everyday life? Do we merely grit our teeth and bear with them? The only difficulty with trying to endure—to wait out the storms—is that with the smaller tempests of life, there's no end. If we're always living for the moment the sea will calm, we will miss the precious moments of the passage.

Our voyage is marked by varied weather. In the midst of dark and threatening clouds comes a sudden rift—an instant of brilliant sunshine—but we tend not to notice God's smile in those warm moments because we're so busy bailing water out of our boats.

Waves, I am discovering, are part of the journey. We can expect them, identify them, learn how to live with them, and let God use them to teach us. God promises us, "When you go through deep waters and great trouble, I will be with you. When you go through rivers of difficulty, you will not drown! When you walk through the fire of oppression, you will not be burned—the flames will not consume you. For I am the Lord your God, your Savior" (Isaiah 43:2-3, TLB). God says, "through the waters," which means there is another side. We go through and we come out. God is in the business of calming storms, quieting winds, and bringing peace.

As I struggled with both the major turbulence and the minor furor, Christ spoke to my heart from Mark 4 as clearly as He spoke to those fishermen. Two truths, like giant sea anchors, descended to steady my boat. First, Christ said, "Why are you afraid? Don't you know I have the power to calm the storms?" Then He said clearly and powerfully, "You are safe with Me anywhere, in every circumstance. My child, you are just as safe in the turbulence before I speak 'Peace' to the waves as you are afterwards because I am with you in the boat."

God takes each individual through just the right combination of waves, storms, and sunshine to learn about Him. He teaches us through our delights and deliverances, as well as through our tears and tempests.

I don't have to live in fear of the storms, whether a tidal wave threatens or many smaller waves constantly rock me. Christ is in control of everything—all the circumstances in my life—and He is also the Captain of my boat!

# CHAPTER EIGHT

# Problems, People, and Priorities

Help Lord . . .
Help Lord . . .
Help Lord . . .

The day began calmly enough. True, it was raining steadily, but that was no problem. Jack was working at home that Monday morning, so I decided to drive over to a local donut shop and get us a treat. It seemed so simple.

I drove into the newly paved shopping center parking lot, spotted a parking place along one side, and pulled into it, not seeing that the cement block that usually prevents cars from going off the asphalt had been pushed into the ditch next to the pavement. The next thing I knew, my car's two front wheels were resting in water a foot deep. No amount of reverse power would budge them.

"I will not take Jack away from his work," I told myself. "I will handle this myself." After purchasing the donuts, I ran home in the rain (only three blocks, but rather wet ones!), called a service station for assistance, and ran back to wait for the tow truck.

Ten minutes later the truck arrived, hitched its chain to the car, and began to pull. In one split second the front wheels of my car turned sideways as they were being pulled out of the ditch. *Bang!* My car hit the brand-new red vehicle parked next to mine. I spent another hour trying to locate the owner and survive the hassle of exchanging information. When I finally got home, the morning was beyond repair. I could only shake my head at the complexity of trivial things.

It wasn't exactly a typical morning. But similar circumstances are not uncommon in most of our lives. Pressures unexpectedly throw our schedules into a tailspin, turn priorities upside down, and chafe the tender "skin" of our lives. The calm surface of our day suddenly becomes choppy. The sky fills with threatening clouds, and our boat begins to rock.

As the waves of pressure slapped alarmingly against my boat, I began looking out at the swells and hollows. Our daughter and her husband were waiting for God's answer to financial needs. Airlines had changed schedules just before a Christmas reunion causing chaos in reservations. One close friend was severely depressed, and another was in the hospital with a heart stoppage. Criticism over various things was causing heartache for Jack. The list went on and on.

I felt panic-stricken!

Then a voice behind me said, "Carole, stop looking at the waves. Turn around and look at Me."

Strange. The waves didn't calm down, but there was a stabilizer I could depend on inside the boat. My need was to focus on Christ.

It's one thing to say I must focus on Christ and not on the waves; it's another to do it! Friends, it isn't easy!

How do you turn your eyes to the Captain when storms threaten your boat? You can begin by identifying what is distracting you.

### Identify the Pressures

I was sailing along through my day just fine when suddenly depression, like a San Francisco fog, settled over my mind. I couldn't figure out what was causing it until Jack started to ask me about my day. In reviewing the three or four nagging criticisms and slurs I'd listened to about people dear to me, in telling of my concern for a sick friend and recalling an unpleasant phone call, in sharing with Jack a letter that told me of the sudden death of a beloved childhood friend who was one of my bridesmaids, I began to identify the pressures that had built up during the day. The final one — the letter concerning my friend's death — had plunged me into the trough of the wave and threatened the stability of my frail craft. I had focused on the storm.

It helped to identify the pressures one by one because that's how we must give them back to God—one at a time. Jack is not always around to help me identify what's disturbing me, but God is. He's always around! And He's always listening. I am never free of pressures, but if I will take the time to ask, He will help me identify them so that I can commit them to Him. It is often the vague pressures, unnoticed and unidentified, that mount up and overwhelm us before we even become aware of the danger.

When I identify and separate the pressures, I can begin to pray about them specifically, one at a time, and ask God for the wisdom to deal with each one.

### Obey God

Some of the pressures that disturb my days stem from the fact that my life is just too complex—a problem that is, in part, my own fault. I know that God can give me creative ideas to eliminate some pressures, even though I may have to make sacrifices. If I learned to say "no" more often, if I trained other people to do a job and planned ahead more efficiently, some pressures would be eliminated. Even little things, like choosing only one accessory color for my wardrobe, could simplify decisions concerning clothes and packing.

Basically, I think the answer lies in realizing that I don't have to do twenty things each day—only one. One day I prayed: "Lord, show me how to simplify. Life is so complex, the ministry so multiple, problems so monumental. I get a handle on one thing only to have three more thrust upon me. I feel so overwhelmed, Lord. Please, simplify my life."

He said, "Dear child, remember the words, 'This one thing I do: I press toward the mark of the high calling of God.' My calling is simple. It is this: Obey Me."

When twenty demands on my time seem to pull me in different directions, I need to remember that truth. I don't have to do one hundred things today. I just have to do one. And that one thing is to do what God tells me to do each moment. Instead of saying, "Lord, I have these tasks planned for today. Please bless me," I need to say, "Lord, what are Your plans for me today? May I be sensitive to Your leading and simply fulfill Your plans one by one."

### Come Away with God
I heard of one great saint who spent two hours alone with God each day. "But," he said, "on very busy days, I spend three hours!" It is when we face the greatest pressures, the most crowded schedules, the days of constant interruptions, that we need even more to come away and spend adequate and precious time with God.

Scripture tells us, "Don't worry about anything; instead, pray about everything; tell God your needs and don't forget to thank him for his answers. If you do this you will experience God's peace, which is far more wonderful than the human mind can understand. His peace will keep your thoughts and your hearts quiet and at rest as you trust in Christ Jesus" (Philippians 4:6-7, TLB).

The pressures of life will always be there. But as I identify them and focus on Christ and His ability to handle them, I am free to relax in His care.


# People

"I've just got to see you for a few minutes." The young woman had started to pass by, then turned around to speak to me in a motel hallway during a conference. Thinking she had a problem or question, I paused and stepped to one side.

She drew close to me, and in an urgent tone said, "You just must get rid of your eyebrows!"

I must have looked as astonished as I felt! (How do you get rid of your eyebrows?) She hastened to add, "Your eyebrows just don't go with your face. They've got to go."

Suddenly it dawned on me what she was talking about. My eyebrows and hair are naturally quite dark, but sun and a recent permanent had turned my hair a lighter-than-usual shade of reddish brown. She apparently thought I was putting on dark eyebrows, which didn't look right to her, but in truth it was my hair that wasn't right.

When she realized her error, she quickly apologized, and I

assured her I wasn't offended. I admired her willingness to risk a relationship in order to help me, even though her approach was a trifle blunt!

However, all day I was terribly conscious of my eyebrows. I couldn't pass a mirror without peering at myself critically. I soon came to the conclusion that something drastic would have to be done, and quickly, about my oddly matched brows and hair.

What small things have the ability to distract and distress us!

Do you realize that the stress of our lives almost always begins with people? I heard one man say, "If it weren't for people I wouldn't have any problems." Smiling inwardly, I had to agree. But what specifically is it about people that causes the storm clouds to gather and the boat to rock? You could answer that question by saying, "Only everything," but let's be specific.

Often stress stems from people's *criticism*. I've been censured for many reasons: from the way I laugh (too loudly), to the way I lead a Bible study (too directly), to the way I listen (too carelessly), to the way I wash a car (too casually). Some of my critics have loved me and truly wanted to help me. They've been willing to risk our relationship in the process. But other critics have been disgruntled or embittered or angry. In any case, criticism hurts.

People's bad *attitudes* can affect us negatively. I appreciate problems shared for prayer, for concern, or because I can meet a particular need. The rough ones are the problems that remain the same day after day, week after week. It's draining to be asked for advice and become emotionally involved with the problem only to have people listen with no intent to do something about it.

And finally there are the *theys* of life. These nameless people can be the most defeating and discouraging of all. Hundreds of times in our lives the faceless *theys* cause us grief and frustration. Have you ever had someone say to you, "*They* don't like the way you're handling things." "*They* are unhappy with the group." "*They* think you should change that department." "*They* think the church is unfriendly." When you ask, "Who is *they*?" the answer is vague and general.

I had to chuckle when I read about the *theys* in Zaccheus's life. In Luke 18:24-25, Christ stated that it was difficult for a rich man to enter the kingdom of God. In the next chapter, He saved one of those very men. Zaccheus was a little man who desperately wanted to see Jesus. He was prevented from doing so by the crowds, so he ran ahead and climbed a sycamore tree (see Luke 19).

I doubt that Zaccheus even thought about how silly he looked—how humiliated he would be if the crowd saw him, which of course is exactly what happened when Jesus stopped and directed the crowd's attention to this rich tax collector up in a tree! Zaccheus was so intent on his purpose, he probably never considered the possibility that his robe might get torn or that he might fall and break his leg. And even if he had taken a moment to think about it, my guess is it wouldn't have changed his course of action. Zaccheus had to see Jesus. When Christ asked to stay at his home, Zaccheus received Him gladly.

And now comes an interesting statement; the *theys* saw it and "*they* all began to grumble" (Luke 19:7, NASB, emphasis added). But Zaccheus didn't let the *theys* in his life bother him at all because his focus was on the Lord. He would not let the *theys* determine his behavior in trying to see Jesus. He didn't allow those who grumbled against him as host and Jesus as guest to stop him from receiving Christ joyously into his home as well as into his heart.

I think we can learn something from this incident. How should we handle the *theys*? Simply by looking at Him—Christ—and ignoring them.

If we're not supposed to ignore the *theys* in our lives—and there is that possibility—Christ will show us that, too. But more often than not, Christ ignored or rebuked them and was sensitive and thoughtful toward individuals.

What can we do when people become problems, when we become harried with the hassles, when we begin to drown under their demands? What can we do with criticism, bad decisions, and ugly attitudes, which are constant waves for most of us?

In order to ride on top of the waves of distress caused by people, I must *love* the very people who cause the problems— love them in a deeper way than I do at the moment.

"How do I do that, Lord?" I prayed one day. "How in the world do I feel compassion for a person who is demanding and inwardly focused, who is a 'taker' all the time? How do I feel compassion— true compassion—for all your children? And how can they possibly feel affection for me, one of the most unlovely of all?"

He seemed to say, "Interesting you should ask," and then 1 Peter 1:22 reached out from the page I was reading, grabbed me by the collar, and none too gently shook me to attention. Peter wrote, "Now that by obedience to the truth you have purified your souls until you *feel* sincere affection towards your brother Christians, love one another whole-heartedly with all your strength" (NEB, emphasis added).

There are people in this world who rub me the wrong way! I don't like them, let alone love them. (Happily, there really aren't many of these.) But 1 Peter 1:22 has the answer, and a very practical one it is. If we obey the Word of God, we are going to be purified to such an extent that we will *feel* (not just talk ourselves into) sincere affection (not a fake caring attitude) for our fellow Christians. That is the secret! The key is obedience.

When God says, "Be ye kind one to another" (Ephesians 4:32, KJV), I can do an act of kindness without necessarily feeling affection. That starts the process.

In addition, God says, "Be understanding" (Ephesians 4:32, AMP). That gets a bit tougher, doesn't it? I can do an act of kindness and not feel anything. So I have to pray for Christ's mind in me in order to be understanding. Because God has promised to answer prayer, He will give me understanding. However, I may still not have any compassion for that person. In 1 Peter 1:22 it says that if I obey the truth, perhaps even *while* I am obeying the truth, I will be purified until I feel sincere affection. What a promise! The feeling will come as I obey the steps God shows me.

God doesn't stop there, however. He says that as I am feeling this sincere affection, I am to do one more thing—obey. And the obedience He requires is to love more! It is an ever-deepening cycle of love. And I am finding that it works.

## Priorities

My eyes were barely open as I wearily staggered down the hall to Eric's room, grumbling to myself, slippers flopping on the cold floor. *Why in the world can't he sleep later than 6:00 A.M.?* I wondered.

But my eight-month-old grandson didn't seem to grasp the logic for sleeping any later on those frigid winter mornings. He lay in his crib, crying for his bottle and needing to be changed.

It was only after he was snuggled close to me and happily drinking his breakfast that I awakened fully enough to appreciate how precious he was and to thank the Lord for the joy of being able to care for him while his parents were away.

I became mother-for-a-week just after Christmas, and I relearned some things I'd forgotten many years before.

I had forgotten how hard it was to have a quiet time when little hands reached constantly for my Bible, or how difficult it was to try to concentrate while keeping one eye out for danger to a small body. I'm sure that I read the same passage in Luke at least twenty-one times and later couldn't have told you what it said.

Spiritually, the week was a disaster, and I discovered some ugly things about myself.

I had been having victory over a particularly trying situation in my life. But gradually, during those post-Christmas days, I found myself getting irritated inside. I lacked compassion and was gritting my teeth and "toughing" it through—just barely, and certainly not triumphantly.

I didn't like myself, what I was feeling, or the selfish, unkind thoughts I was thinking about the ones involved in the problem. However, I didn't connect my obnoxious attitude to my lack of time with God until Eric had gone home. Then I took time to ask God about the cause of my abominable disposition, and it became very clear what had happened. I had allowed my priorities to get all mixed up. As a result, an unloving attitude had come to the forefront.

When I went back to the passage in Luke 17:1-10, which I had been trying to read with some comprehension during the week with Eric, I almost laughed out loud! God had tried to say something to me, but I had been too preoccupied to listen. This is the portion I was trying to read:

> Jesus said to his disciples: "Things that cause people to sin are bound to come, but woe to that person through whom they come. It would be better for him to be thrown into the

sea with a millstone tied around his neck than for him to cause one of these little ones to sin. So watch yourselves.

"If your brother sins, rebuke him, and if he repents, forgive him. If he sins against you seven times in a day, and seven times comes back to you and says, 'I repent,' forgive him."

The apostles said to the Lord, "Increase our faith!"

He replied, "If you have faith as small as a mustard seed, you can say to this mulberry tree, 'Be uprooted and planted in the sea,' and it will obey you.

"Suppose one of you had a servant plowing or looking after the sheep. Would he say to the servant when he comes in from the field, 'Come along now and sit down to eat'? Would he not rather say, 'Prepare my supper, get yourself ready and wait on me while I eat and drink; after that you may eat and drink'? Would he thank the servant because he did what he was told to do? So you also, when you have done everything you were told to do, should say, 'We are unworthy servants; we have only done our duty.'"

Now this isn't an easy passage to understand, so maybe I have a good excuse for having read it twenty-one times without understanding it! But when I was able to concentrate as I read it, and prayed for understanding, God gave me some.

Christ is telling His disciples some hard things about not causing people to stumble, rebuking them if they sin, and being ready to forgive them seven times a day—every time they ask for forgiveness in true repentance—if necessary.

The disciples tried to get the responsibility off themselves and on Christ. In answer to His admonition to forgive someone seven times a day, they responded, "Increase our faith!"

When the disciples asked to have their faith increased, Christ answered, "If you have faith as small as a mustard seed, you can say to this mulberry tree, 'Be uprooted and planted in the sea,' and it will obey you."

It seems He is saying, "Friends, it isn't the amount of your faith that is your problem. You need faith only the size of a mustard seed to be able to uproot trees."

No, faith isn't the topic here. Obedience is. Christ goes on to say that a servant isn't rewarded for doing his or her job. It is expected that she will do what she ought to do. The reward will come later. Her job now is to obey. "So you also, when you have done everything you were told to do, should say, 'We are unworthy servants; we have only done our duty'" (Luke 17:10).

My personal paraphrase of that passage reads something like this: "Friends, you are to forgive. Let's not quibble about having the faith necessary to do it—you have all you need. Now your job is simply to *do* it! And do it without looking for extra reward. Your job is to obey Me in everything, including forgiving others. And don't be proud of doing what is your job."

As I reflected on the two weeks of entertaining at Christmas and the week of Eric-sitting, I think I expected a spiritual pat on the back—I expected to come in from the field and "sit down to eat" (verse 7). In other words, I wanted to be rewarded and complimented by God for doing my job. My mental conversation with God went like this: "It was a lot of work, wasn't it, Lord? I did it heartily as unto You (well, most of the time), didn't I? Then don't I deserve a letter of recommendation? A bit of rest? A 'thank you' in my spirit?"

But I had to answer myself: "No. In the first place, I didn't even do what You said. I didn't fellowship deeply and daily with You. I didn't keep my priorities straight. I was irritated inside and ugly outside."

I had gotten it backwards! The whole time in itself had been one great big bonus from God. It had been a delightful Christmas in every way. But even if I had maintained my priorities and had a good response to the situation, it would only have been what God commanded me to do. My attitude of obedience should have been like the servant of old: "We are unworthy servants; we have only done our duty" (Luke 17:10).

I am discovering that if my priorities are not in order, I can lose the sense of Christ's presence in the process of serving Him. I have to keep Christ in a preeminent position in my life.

In my own quest to be mastered by the Master, I am saying, "Yes, I am willing to take the time. But where is it?" There are days when my time gets pressed down and pushed together until I begin to dread what's coming next. On one such day I wrote:

The demands of my life—small, petty, inconsequential—are running my life. I seem to have lost all control. I am not running my life. Life is running me. I don't like it.

"Wait a moment, child," God said. "You have given your time to Me. I control the interruptions, the demands, and even the seemingly inconsequential details. Truly, there are no such things. I am not just Lord of your life but the Lord of your moments. Trust Me."

If I truly give my time to God, then He will control it. Doing what seems to be inconsequential becomes an act of obedience if I do it as unto Him. The irritating interruptions can be handled "heartily as unto the Lord and not unto men" if I really believe God is in control. I must turn my time over to Him and know that in His sovereignty He can control every minute of my day.

## FOR REFLECTION

1. Problems, people, and priorities can take our eyes off Jesus. Which do you struggle with the most? Why?
2. Are you keeping your time with God and your relationship with Him your top priority? If not, what can you do about it?
3. What are some ways you can keep your focus on the Father and not the storm?

# CHAPTER NINE
# Pain

*Help Lord . . .*
*Help Lord . . .*
*Help Lord . . .*

I asked Jack to do it. I was too much of a coward. Muff had been part of our family for almost thirteen years. But now a giant tumor hindered movement and caused her so much pain that we decided to put her to sleep.

I told myself, *There is so much human misery in the world. Muff is just a dog, and she's had a good, happy life. I will not cry.* But I did.

Jack left on a trip overseas shortly after Muff went to wherever good dogs go, and for the first time ever I was absolutely alone in our home. When the wind made scratching sounds at the patio door, I automatically headed for it to let Muff in. Every time I rounded the corner by the refrigerator, I glanced down to see if Muff's water dish needed refilling. And then a small pang somewhere in the area of my heart made me wince. There was no more Muff.

Aren't you glad Jesus knows about our little hurts, too?

Sometimes it's the gathering of many tiny torments that threatens to inundate us. Little hurts that skin our knees and make them just barely bleed can be pesky to deal with. Those wee pains and big problems can weigh us down and keep us from soaring with God. One day I was contemplating this and wrote:

Her thoughts said, "Father, I'm not soaring today. Help me."

The Father said, "Daughter, soaring is not always flying high above the world, a tiny speck between the sun and the earth. Sometimes you soar only two feet above the ground. It is soaring just the same."

She realized then that problems are not always seen from afar when you soar with God. At times they are so close that except for the wind of the Spirit bearing up her wings, she would even be entangled in the thorns or crash against the rocks.

Have you ever gotten a blister on your little toe? No big thing—just a chafing, sore blister. Your shoe rubs against it; even your slipper causes friction. It's not enough agony to keep you from walking, but it's constantly there.

So it is with the small aches of life. They are so constantly there, and they hurt us until the hurt becomes a part of the throb of life itself. They can be physical aches, such as a nagging backache or tennis elbow. They can be emotional aches, such as a valued friend moving away, the death of a pet, children leaving for college. They can be mental aches, such as the menopausal symptom of not being able to remember things. They can be spiritual aches, such as a dry time in your walk with God.

What do you do about the tiny hurts? What helps you handle the small distresses of life? Sometimes it's easier to discuss what doesn't help ease the discomfort—at least it is for me.

It doesn't help to look at people who are worse off than I am. Microscopic as the torment is, it's real to me. In Joni Eareckson's book *A Step Further* she writes:

> Some months after my accident, I started to notice that the small everyday difficulties my friends and relatives experienced—broken fingernails, dental bills, hay fever, and dented car fenders—were every bit as real to them as my immobility was to me. It began to strike me that there is something universal about suffering. In the first place, everyone experiences it; no one is exempt. But in the

second place, no matter how much or how little one must endure, everyone finds suffering unpleasant. An irksome housefly can momentarily rob a person of joy every bit as much as a broken leg in a cast.[1]

It doesn't help to play a martyr role. A suffer-in-silence attitude shrieks loudly through our sighs and downcast expression and is unpleasant for those around us.

It doesn't help to commiserate with a friend who is having problems, too. This can become a "Can-you-top-this?" time of magnifying our plight through introspection, examination, and dissection of the pain and the reasons for it.

On the other hand, sometimes it does help me to take a friend to lunch, have my hair done, have a date with my husband (this gets at least three stars), begin an interesting project, watch a funny television show or movie, play a game of tennis, take a swim, go for a walk, or do something for someone else to make them happy.

These suggestions may help smooth away the wrinkles of the pain, but what will work for sure? I am discovering that it's not the little pains of life that defeat us as much as it's how we view them. The best way we can handle them is to see them as God's chisel to fashion our lives. Part of the answer to how we can change our attitude toward the small agonies lies in our approach to life itself. Is it negative or positive?

For instance, I can bemoan Muff's death, or I can thank God for thirteen years of enjoyable companionship.

I can gripe about my dented fender, or I can praise God because no one was hurt in the accident.

I can be disgusted with the rain that spoiled a picnic, or I can be glad for the needed moisture.

A positive spirit is not developed overnight. It's something we have to work on and pray for. I wonder how many of us ask God for a positive, thankful attitude?

Another part of the answer to the small aches of life is *focus.* Our attention cannot be on the pain. It must be placed on the Master. Elisabeth Elliot reminded me of this truth in her book *Love Has a Price Tag.*

The Bible does not speak of problems. As Corrie ten Boom says, "God has no problems, only plans." We ought to think not of problems but of purpose. . . .

Life is full of things we can't do anything about, but which we are supposed to do something with. "He himself endured a cross and thought nothing of its shame because of the joy." A very different story from the one which would have been written if Jesus had been prompted by the spirit of our own age: "Don't just endure the cross—*think* about it, talk about it, share it, express your gut-level feelings, get in touch with yourself, find out who you are, define the problem, analyze it, get counseling, get the experts' opinions, discuss solutions, work through it." Jesus endured. He thought *nothing* of the shame. The freedom, the freshness of that valiant selflessness is like a strong wind. How badly such a wind is needed to sweep away the pollution of our self-preoccupation![2]

The more we feed an attitude and allow it to prevail, the harder it is to see life any other way. God tells us that we are what we think. "As he thinketh in his heart, so *is* he" (Proverbs 23:7, KJV). Phillips Brooks put it this way: "Life is too short to nurse one's misery. Hurry across the lowlands that you may spend more time on the mountaintops!"[3]

Finally, when the little hurts persist, the action that helps me far more than anything else is to pour it all out to God. Psalm 62:8 has been a practice of my life: "Trust in him at all times, O people; pour out your hearts to him, for God is our refuge."

When I go to the Lord and begin to pour out my heart to Him—telling Him all of my frustrations, irritations, complaints, and hurts—I find the "healing balm of Gilead" that begins to soothe my wounds. Not only do I know He understands, which in itself helps a great deal, but He can do something about it. He can give me insight as to what effect His chisel can have on my life. He can help me see the situation from His point of view. He can give me a spirit of thankfulness. He can bind my wounds. He cups my hurting life in His gentle, caring hands and whispers, "Peace."

**FOR REFLECTION**

1. Corrie ten Boom said that "God has no problems, only plans." How does God's perspective affect your view of pain?
2. Think of areas of pain in your life. How can you pour them out to God?

# CHAPTER TEN

# Worthless Things

Help Lord . . .
Help Lord . . .
Help Lord . . .

I've said before that when God wants to teach us a special lesson, He seems to speak from everywhere.

A certain admonition began coming at me from all sides! In doing a Bible study on experiencing God's attributes, we had just come to a chapter on God's holiness. A dynamic message on the subject of holiness had been given that very week at a conference I attended. To top off the week, a friend's book called *The Pursuit of Holiness* had just come off the press, and I was reading it every night before I went to sleep.

I didn't even have to ask the Lord twice if He wanted to give me some instruction on holiness. But what did He want to teach me?

I learned long ago that God does not deal with me in generalities but in specifics. In His Word He says, "Be holy, because I am holy" (1 Peter 1:16), which is a comprehensive, sweeping command. Then for me He adds, "Especially in this one area over here, Carole." Later I may realize He's saying, "There's another one we need to work on."

I am so grateful that God doesn't back His holiness truck into my small back yard and dump the complete load on one little seedbed. Instead, He precisely measures the potting soil, mixes in the exact amount of fertilizer, cultivates the new growth with love, and carefully pulls out the weeds, one by one.

At this point, God was busy pulling some weeds in my life. As I began to ask Him for His precise instruction, Psalm 101:2-3 stood out: "I will walk within my house in the integrity of my heart. I will set no worthless thing before my eyes" (NASB).

Jack had been overseas for more than a week. Coming home to an empty house in the evening made me long for a voice—any voice. So the minute the evening news came on, I turned on the television. Whether or not anything worthwhile followed the news, I didn't turn off the television even if I was reading or in another part of the house.

That was the first thing God spoke to my heart about—the many "worthless things" I was setting before my eyes—or ears, at any rate. I'm not saying there isn't any value in relaxing with a good television program. I'm saying there's a lot on television that isn't only worthless, it's bad. And even when the program may be morally acceptable, it can be a "worthless thing" if God wants me to be doing something else.

So God led me to go through the television guide that came in the Sunday newspaper and mark all the worthwhile programs. I wouldn't necessarily watch all of them; but while Jack was away I would be careful not to have the television on if I had not marked a program during that time slot. I found God filling my house with His presence in a new way so that I didn't need that human voice filling the living room.

There was more to learn. Much more.

I found that I was setting worthless things before my thoughts as well. The minute I said that, you probably equated worthless things with evil thoughts, didn't you? I do have to battle thoughts of envy, selfishness, jealousy, and self-pity, but these are not the kind of thoughts God was speaking to me about just then. It was the worthless ones—thoughts that are totally without redeeming value.

He began to talk to me about the "what ifs" of my life. At that point, they were running something like this: *What if Joye doesn't live until her daughter's wedding in a few months? What if she's too sick to take part in the ceremony? What if I'm overseas when she needs me?* Like a battering ram, the "what ifs" slammed against my peace, leaving me half-paralyzed with fear.

"What ifs" never do one iota of good. They're not only crippling, they're utterly worthless. If I believe God is in control of every situation, then I won't give time to the "what ifs," for they are a form of worry, and worry is a lack of trust, or sin.

I had to pray then and claim Psalm 34:4: "I sought the Lord, and he answered me; he delivered me from all my fears." I prayed, "Lord, deliver me from the 'what ifs' of my thoughts. May I not set those worthless things before my spiritual eyes. Deliver me not only from the fear that comes from these thoughts, but deliver me from the cause of the fear as well. The cause seems to be a lack of truly trusting you. Thank You."

You will never live this twenty-four hours again. You can never reclaim this day. The time spent on worthless things can never be recovered. God's command is abundantly clear: "Be very careful, then, how you live — not as unwise, but as wise, making the most of every opportunity because the days are evil. Therefore do not be foolish, but understand what the Lord's will is" (Ephesians 5:15-17). Do you know what the will of God is? It is to make the most of your time!

Good things at the wrong time can be worthless things, such as spending days in wonderful causes at the expense of the family; taking time to study when God wants you to be laboring, or laboring when God wants you to study. Soap operas, garage sales, hobbies, gourmet cooking — anything that interferes with God's plan for your time today can be a worthless thing.

There are numerous other items God is going to tell me are worthless things for me. I expect it will be a continuing lesson all my life. But oh, how I want to be open — to walk within my house (and outside of it, too) with integrity of heart — to erase those "worthless things" from the blackboard of my mind!

### FOR REFLECTION

1. What are some of the "worthless things" in your life? Why are they worthless?
2. Many of us suffer from the "what ifs" of life. How can you surrender those fears to God?
3. How can you remain open to God's teaching about worthless things?

# CHAPTER ELEVEN

# Personalities — Mainly My Own!

Help Lord . . .
Help Lord . . .
Help Lord . . .

I was singing as I worked in the kitchen—enthusiastically and slightly off-key. Jack came in, put his arm around me, and observed, "Some women can cook. Some women can lead Bible studies. Some women can grow plants. Some women can sing." He paused, and a teasing twinkle flickered in his eyes. Then he commented wryly, "Oh well, three out of four isn't bad!"

I can laugh at my inability to make beautiful music, but other defects in my life are no laughing matter! Jack so wonderfully accepts me, with my idiosyncrasies and faults, that he has helped me to accept myself and also see how God accepts me in an even greater way. Still, there are many things about myself I just don't like. Truthfully, the personality I have the most trouble with is my own!

One of the things I like least about myself is my propensity to have to say something (usually the wrong thing) when there's an uncomfortable silence in a conversation. Because of this inclination, I totally identify with Peter and his reaction to the astonishing wonder of the Transfiguration in Mark 9:1-13. When he saw Moses and Elijah talking to a transfigured Christ, Peter was awed, terrified, thunderstruck, and he "did not know what to say."

As I read that passage, I thought, *Didn't know what to say? Who asked him to say anything?* Yet Peter had to blurt out something, so he suggested that three tabernacles be built to honor the three who were conversing. In my nervousness, I, like Peter, think I've got to answer when no one has asked!

The incredible thing about this incident is that God the Father didn't rebuke Peter. Neither did Christ shake His head in anger at Peter's remark. Instead, God used Peter's inane suggestion to point out dramatically that Christ was His beloved Son. When Peter looked about, after suggesting that three tabernacles be erected, Christ alone stood on that mountain. God thundered from heaven, "This is my Son, whom I love. Listen to Him!"

The lesson God whispered to me as I studied this incident was that I'm to keep my eyes on Jesus rather than on my own disheartening tendencies. I am to remember that God not only understands those propensities but, at times, graciously uses them. My task is to focus only on Jesus. When I see Him clearly with my spiritual eyes, I can forget myself and those things I don't like about myself.

Numerous articles, books, and people tell us that we must love ourselves in order to love others or even love Christ. Phrases such as *a healthy self-image*, *self-love*, *self-acceptance*, and *I'm okay* dot the landscape of our lives like mounds of hay in a farmer's field. We, as individuals and as a society, are reaching out for a good self-image, a feeling of worth, a sense of genuine acceptance from those around us. We want to be liked and loved and to know that we are. Surely there's nothing wrong with that.

Or is there? Has giving attention to our self-image detracted from giving attention to the image of Christ? Has our search for self-worth blocked our view of the worthiness of Jesus? Has our desire to be loved and accepted overcome our desire to know God?

I have a feeling that our focus has been on the wrong object. We've put self in our sight and blocked the Savior from view. It's no wonder our search for Him gets more and more frantic.

I am becoming increasingly convinced that the answer to a healthy view of myself lies not in reading books and learning formulas by which I grow to love myself; it lies in experiencing fully a God who sees me as worthy to be loved. In knowing His love, I feel loved. In seeing His beauty, I don't think of myself as beautiful or not beautiful; I stop thinking of myself at all so that I might better fill my heart with Him. But in everyday life, that isn't easy.

One time a friend of mine, who was quite overweight, came to visit. Without thinking, I used a phrase I frequently heard as a child. I said, "Sit down, friend, and take the load off your feet." As soon as it was out of my mouth, I realized the embarrassing implication of my remark. But what could I say then to make amends?

Afterwards, I could have given myself a pep talk something like this: "Now Carole, it's okay. (It wasn't!) You don't often make thoughtless remarks. (Oh yes, you do!) You are really a great person. (Who says?) You must love yourself. (Yes, but how?)"

Frankly, I don't think that would have helped much. And to keep thinking about my blunder wouldn't help either. But to talk to my Father about it, to ask Him to help my friend not to be hurt by my thoughtlessness, to ask Him to deliver my thoughts from dwelling on myself and my inadequacies, and then to set my mind on God who loves me anyhow helps me to experience a feeling of acceptance and even joy in being me.

So how can I alleviate the trouble I have with myself? Perhaps we could call it the FACTS principle.

- ⑥ Focus on a God who loves me beyond my comprehension
- ⑥ Accept my idiosyncrasies with humor, knowing that God can even use them for His glory or change them as He will
- ⑥ Concentrate on His Book more than on self-help books
- ⑥ Totally desire to know God better than anyone else
- ⑥ Study Him through life's experiences

I have many rough edges that God wants chiseled away. My responsibility is to let Him do His work unhindered—to try not to resist His sculpting tools. Other than that, I can relax and rest in the fact that God made me the way He wanted me. This may not be the way I would wish or others would desire. But as a unique member of the body of Christ, I have a special task—an obligation to be exactly what I was created to be. I want the fragrance of my life to be sweet, not because of what I am at this moment but because of what God is making of me.

## FOR REFLECTION

1. What are some of your "disheartening tendencies?"
2. How can you keep your eyes on God rather than on your personality faults?
3. What are some ways you can apply the FACTS principle to your life?

# CHAPTER TWELVE

# The Tidal Wave

Help Lord . . .
Help Lord . . .
Help Lord . . .

I sat with my eyes closed against the glare of the early spring sun warm upon my face. Idly I stirred the ice in the Coke glass resting on the stone table of the McDonald's patio, delaying my return to the hospital.

If the strangers sitting nearby noticed me at all, they undoubtedly saw a rather normal, if weary looking, woman. Had some giant hand turned me, glovelike, inside out, those people would have been shocked to see the internal devastation and debris left from hurricane winds running before a tidal wave in my life.

Fortunately for most of us, tidal waves do not come often. But when they start to build and swell to monstrous proportions, they have the capacity to flood the very foundation of our faith and even capsize our boat.

I kept telling myself that I didn't have to fear the tidal wave; Christ could and would dissolve it before it had a chance to break. I repeated over and over that the tidal wave was not the problem. Ordinarily, it was those little waves and leaks that I had to live with daily that threatened to swamp me. Nonetheless, as the tidal wave swelled, for weeks—months—I felt like I was drowning.

It was only two months after my mother died of a massive

stroke that Joye was diagnosed with acute lymphatic leukemia. After an initial four months of being critically ill, God gave her a wonderful yearlong remission. Then the illness hit in another form—leukemic meningitis. After that, the disease, like an unmanned bobsled, careened downward, rampantly out of control.

I shared what God taught me in those initial months of Joye's illness in *Lord, Teach Me Wisdom*, which became the first part of this book. I finished writing that while Joye was in remission. During that year God miraculously supplied all of us with His abundant, supernatural grace. I knew the tidal wave of Joye's death was forming somewhere, but God's grace was so real, so strong, that I didn't experience then the gamut of emotions to follow.

Our family will never forget Christmas 1978. Joye had a relapse in August, and another one in early December. Chemotherapy seemed to be of temporary help, and she began another series of injections early that month. All of us were praying that the family reunion at our home in Colorado would take place. And God answered in providing alternate plane reservations when a strike suspended flights on a national airline; in giving us flights that were problem-free (Joye's family arrived just before a major snowstorm closed airports across the country and went home just before another snowstorm!); in Joye's ability to talk and fellowship with all her loved ones; in keeping her nausea at bay so she could enjoy the food and fun. She was weak, of course, and spent most of the time lying on the couch, but we all knew it was a miracle that she was there at all. We had a wonderful last family Christmas together.

Another relapse occurred in March, just before her daughter's wedding. I flew east to help with the wedding plans in which Joye was unable to participate. She lay on the hide-a-bed in the living room, presents and guests surrounding her, with the ebb and flow of laughter and chatter splashing against her pain and sickness. She was incredibly weak yet determined to see Melody married. God enabled her to get up just thirty minutes before the wedding ceremony to dress. She had lost all her beautiful hair from the chemotherapy, but a friend who was a hairdresser had styled her wig to look so like her own hair that we could hardly tell it wasn't. God suspended her wrenching vomiting and, with head high, she walked serenely down the aisle as mother of the bride. Immediately after the wedding photos were taken she returned to bed, but later she remembered details I couldn't recall. Although her body was weak, her spirit was able to be 100 percent there.

Two days later, pain forced her back into the hospital. In two weeks she stabilized and was able to return home. We hoped she was being given another spell of freedom from the pain and weakness.

Jack and I were due to leave in the middle of May for a ten-week ministry trip overseas that had been planned for over a year. We were excited about the opportunity, and it was one I knew God wanted for us. Yet it was inconceivable to me that God would not permit me to be with Joye when she went home to heaven. I felt confident that God would either heal Joye, stabilize her condition for some months, or take her to heaven before our trip began. But He didn't.

I flew east to see her in early May. Her condition was deteriorating rapidly and I longed to be of help if I could. She needed someone to be with her at the hospital during her waking hours because she was so disoriented at times that she couldn't call the nurse for help. Many times she lacked the strength to feed herself. Her husband and daughter were working during the day, and I was thankful I could drive in early to help her with breakfast. I felt grateful to be able to hold her and pray when the waves of pain and nausea came. I was glad just to sit quietly as she slept when the shots gave her momentary relief.

I had never seen anyone suffer so intensely, let alone someone I cared for deeply. I felt like I was drowning in her pain. I was consumed by it, and at times I felt angry at God, who could prevent it but didn't. I cried to Him day after day to take her, to deliver her, to do *something*.

I read everything I could find. Joyce Landorf's *The Mourning Song* was a consolation, though the first two chapters were so heavy that I had to put it away at first and come back to it later in God's special time. C. S. Lewis's *A Grief Observed* made me realize that even a spiritual giant sometimes screams and rails at God in pain and grief. *Where Is God When It Hurts?* by Philip Yancey, and *A Step Further* by Joni Eareckson and Steve Estes gave me some insight. But I still felt like I was being inundated, and my feelings were out of control.

Writing down some of those feelings was therapeutic. I had no intention of ever sharing them, but in order to describe my personal encounter with a tidal wave, I'm going to include a part of what I wrote during Joye's illness.

APRIL 26, 1979

For some time I have been struggling—hurting—wondering—mentally thrashing over the "whys" of Joye's pain and long-suffering in the light of God's lovingkindness. Last night God used a secular book (The *Reader's Digest* condensed version of *War and Remembrance*, by Herman Wouk) to flip on a light in my understanding.

In the story, an agnostic Jew turns again to his religious heritage when he is imprisoned by the Germans. As several thousand of his countrymen are being shipped to an unknown fate, he lectures to them from the Book of Job. After describing the exchange between God and Satan, which preceded Job's suffering, this Jewish teacher says: "His [Job's] comforters maintain that since one Almighty God rules the universe, it must make sense. Therefore Job must have sinned. The missing piece is only what his offense was.

"In round after round of soaring argument, Job fights back. The missing piece must be with God, not with him. He is as religious as they are. He knows that the Almighty exists, that the universe must make sense. But he knows now that it does not in fact always make sense; that there is no guarantee of good fortune for good behavior; that crazy injustice is part of this life. His religion demands that he assert his innocence, *otherwise he will be profaning God's name*! He will be conceding that the Almighty can botch one man's life; and if God can do that, the whole universe is a botch, and he is not an Almighty God. That, Job will never concede. He wants an answer.

"He gets an answer! God himself speaks at last out of a roaring storm. '*Who are you to call me to account? Can you hope to understand why or how I do anything? Were you there at the Creation? Can you comprehend the infinite wonders of*

*existence? You, a worm that lives a few moments, and dies?'*
"My friends, Job has won! God has conceded Job's main
point, that *the missing piece is with him*! God claims only
that his reason is beyond Job."[1]

The words seemed to flash in neon: "The missing piece is with
him." In my life there have been a number of missing pieces—
things I could not understand concerning the ways of God. But
almost without exception, after the experience, God has given
glimmers of the "why" and the reason for it in my life or the lives
of others. Here was another giant missing piece I had been trying
to find. "Where is it, God?" I had cried. God has answered, "Dear
child, it is right here in my hand. Can you trust Me with it?" I think
that in future days God may give me some further glimmers of
understanding about the deep things He has done in my own heart.
He may reveal to me those people who have been touched by Him
through this suffering. But now I know. The missing piece is with
Him! And yes, I can leave it there.

MAY 1, 1979
O Father, I don't seem to be able to hear You.
> Your voice is far away and dim.
> My belief seems shattered upon the wasteplaces within
> > my heart.

> Dear Child, I will rebuild the wasteplaces.
> Leave your trembling, unbelieving, dim-of-hearing
> > heart with Me.
> Trust Me. Just keep on trusting Me. Trust Me. Trust
> > Me.

MAY 10, 1979. JOYE'S HOSPITAL ROOM.
God just washed the earth's face with a refreshing shower.
Fragrant teardrops of moisture cling to lilacs massed against
the backdrop of brownstone houses and narrow alleyways.
Blue is again dimpling the gray clouds, and now and then a
ray of sunshine momentarily touches the window.
     Inside the sterile hospital room I listen to my sister's

labored breathing. She mumbles a few unintelligible words in her drugged sleep and then falls back into her world of half-sleep. I am glad she has a respite from pain for these few minutes.

I am torn and bleeding inside, yet at the same time supported and strengthened. The ambiguity of my feelings leaves me weary—oh, so weary.

Tomorrow I will leave her. I have faced the terrible fact that I may never see her on earth again.

The doctor says she could go suddenly or she could live for weeks or even months. Our overseas trip begins in four days. I have total peace in one part of my heart that God has been in those plans and that He wants me to go. My sister and her husband have urged me to go.

The other part of my heart is crying, despairing. It is accusing as well. "Deserter!" it cries. "How can you leave? Remember when she held out her hand—oh, her thin, weak, beautiful hand—and said, 'I love you?' And when you responded in the same way, she said, 'I can't say or do much, but it is so good to have someone here.' And now you won't be there. Won't be there to put a cool cloth on her head when her body writhes in pain. Won't be there to tend to her needs. Won't *be* there!"

A hundred questions prick my heart like fiery needles, but the big one is *Why*? Three times the doctor has said, "She's deteriorating." Three times I have come to sit with her, to make some feeble efforts to help. And now I'm leaving her. Yes, leaving her in the capable, loving hands of husband, daughter, and friends, but leaving her nonetheless.

Why, Lord? When Your timing has been so perfect, so kind in Mother's homegoing—in Dad's—why are You not allowing me to say a personal goodbye—to be with Joye when she is ushered into Your presence? Yet to ask You to leave her here during the time I will be gone—oh no, Lord! She has suffered too long already. I cry for You to deliver her from these waves of agony which seem to engulf her. No, I'd rather she be at peace, singing and laughing in heaven, than waiting for me to say farewell.

Oh, God. Thank You for Your patience with my questions and the fury of my sometimes angry thoughts. Thank You for understanding my trampled, downtrodden heart. Thank You for loving me even when I'm screaming and hurling angry questions at You. Thank You for being my Rock, my Fortress, my Shield, my Help, and I know at last, my Deliverer—and Joye's!

The hardest thing I have ever had to do was to say goodbye to Joye the morning I flew home to prepare for our overseas trip. Before I left, God opened a door of opportunity to share with all the regular and student nurses on the cancer floor. I had been asked to speak to them on how we were dealing internally with Joye's imminent death.

My mind was so muddled, the only thing I could do was to say a desperate, "Help, Lord," as I considered what to say. Immediately, God brought to my mind His words, "And these three remain: faith, hope and love. But the greatest of these is love" (1 Corinthians 13:13). In a few moments God had given me not just the outline of what to say, but the meat as well. So I slipped from Joye's room while she was sleeping and shared with those nurses and aides what I knew was the only possible way Joye and her family were responding to her dying.

I told them we could accept it because of the truth of the concepts expressed in 1 Corinthians 13:13. We could look at death head-on because of our faith. Not general faith, but specific faith; not in a religion, but in a Person—Jesus Christ. As children both Joye and I, though raised in a Christian family, knew that a secondhand relationship with God didn't count. It had to be firsthand or it was nothing. We knew that we were separated from God by our sins (our sibling fights were enough to convince us that we fell far short of God's perfection). But God, in His love, had provided the way back into fellowship with Himself. In justice He had pronounced the sentence—death for sin—and then in love He had paid that very penalty Himself (see Romans 3:23, 6:23, and 5:8). Jesus Christ—God Himself—died in our place.

It had been made clear to us that the choice of whether to receive His gift or reject Him was ours alone. We understood that we were not judged for our commission of sin (Christ died for all sin—past, present, and future) or our condition (we were born sinful, but Christ also took care of that). We were judged on the basis of our choice, or response, to Christ's sacrifice.

Early in her life, Joye had made that decision. She had received Christ into her life. Her faith in Him and her acceptance of Him had made her a child of God. So, first of all, we were able to accept her illness and coming death because we had faith in a personal, living, loving God.

I told the nurses that we had many questions about why God would allow such suffering, but we knew He had the answers to those questions and that someday, though perhaps not until we reached heaven, He would tell us the "whys."

We also have hope, not an "I-hope-so" hope but a sure hope, that this life is just a minute part of real life—eternal life. Life on earth is a training ground for eternity. When Joye dies, her life doesn't end; her body just stops functioning for a while. Knowing that the separation is temporary gives us true hope.

Finally, I said, we are able to survive these days because of love—love of family, friends, and beautiful, serving nurses. I was able to thank them personally for all the kind, loving care they had extended to Joye, her family, and me. I told them it was a big factor in our handling Joye's illness.

I concluded by saying, "But the greatest of these is love." I explained that God's love in extending forgiveness, caring, acceptance, and an inheritance that is incorruptible and undefiled is reserved in heaven for Joye—for me—for every person who becomes His child by receiving God's gift of eternal life through Christ.

I returned to Joye's room and, weak as she was, she wanted to hear what I'd said and how the nurses had responded. She was happy that God had again used her illness as an open door to present the Lord. We prayed together and I told her that if I didn't see her again down here, I'd see her up there. I asked her to give Mom and Dad a big hug for me. Her faint smile was tender. We kissed goodbye and I walked out of her room.

I am writing this through tears. I may never be able to think about that moment without crying.

Every word I shared with those nurses was true. Yet as I began my flight home, I felt as though my face had been pushed into the mud of pain until it filled my nose and mouth and eyes and ears — until I swallowed great gulps of it and it had spread to every pore and cell of my body, mind, and spirit. I had lived with pain, loathing it, until there were no screams left. No tears. No prayers. Nothing.

Silently, in utter desperation, I cried out to God. "Oh Lord, where are You? Help me."

It was then He spoke one word. He said, "Let."

"Let?" I shrieked internally. "What do you mean, 'Let'?"

I heard Him say distinctly to my heart, "Let Me heal you. Let Me take the shattered slivers and put you back together. Let Me give you peace. Let Me give you trust. Let Me. Let."

All the "let" verses I knew began to flash like lightning in the dark night of my mind: "Let the peace of Christ rule in your hearts" (Colossians 3:15); "Let the word of Christ dwell in you richly . . . with all wisdom" (Colossians 3:16); "Let us hold unswervingly to the hope we profess, for he who promised is faithful" (Hebrews 10:23); "Let us then approach the throne of grace with confidence, so that we may receive mercy and find grace to help us in our time of need" (Hebrews 4:16). "Do not let your hearts be troubled. Trust in God; trust also in me" (John 14:1).

It was a moment of revelation. I saw clearly what had happened. With one part of me I had steadily and constantly cried out to God for His help, His comfort, His sustaining grace. With another part of me I had been punishing God for hurting my sister (that was how I viewed it at the time).

Unconsciously, my punishing had taken the form of not allowing Him to comfort me. My mind whispered, "Why should I be comforted when Joye is hurting so?" My punitive measures took the form of keeping Him at arm's length and being unresponsive to His love.

Now He was saying, "Let." And I knew exactly what He meant. Silently I cried, "Oh, Lord, I want to let You break down the walls of my anger at the pain and grief — and at You — and let You heal me."

At that moment, God spoke to the tidal wave that so long had threatened me. His personal pronouncement was clearly given: "Peace! Be still!" and the tidal wave rose, poised at the crest for a timeless moment, and subsided without a ripple.

I felt it then. A little bubble, very faint but very definitely there, gurgled somewhere—a bubble of His joy. It had been missing for some months, but I knew it would return in time to full-scale rhythmic bubbling. I was to drink of each day's joy during our forthcoming trip, even as the specter of sorrow hovered over the edge of the cup. And God would enable me to do that as I let Him.

Our daughter Lynn reached us by phone in Stuttgart, Germany, two weeks into our trip and told us that Joye had gone home on Memorial Day, 1979. God had privileged her husband Fred, son Mike, and daughter Melody to be with her. Even though Joye was comatose, the three gathered around her had been praying and singing all morning. About 1:30 P.M., after they had finished the song "Alleluia," Joye went to heaven—no doubt singing the second chorus!

No, I wasn't there. On the day of her memorial service, Jack and I were speaking to couples in the hills of Ghana. And God enabled me to smile! Two-and-a-half weeks earlier, high above the earth, God had spoken His personal "Peace" to my heart.

I have learned some things from the forming of the tidal wave. As I've reflected on what to do when a giant wave threatens, several things come to mind.

If we are forewarned, we prepare. Of course we get out of its way if we can. If not, we batten down the hatches, make our ship strong, and throw out the sea anchor. If we are not forewarned— and the majority of life's tidal waves hit without the kind of warning I had with Joye—we need to be in a constant state of readiness, with our boats sturdy and in repair. Now, how do we prepare ourselves spiritually?

A phrase that has always been a challenge to me is "As now, so then." As I am living my life right now, so I will be in old age, or when trouble comes. Do I want to be a woman of the Word and of prayer, one who walks closely with God? As I am right now— today—so it is likely my life will be ten years from now. Therefore, I cannot let a day go by when I am not giving time to God's Word in study, reading, memorizing, and meditating on Him. It is in these ways that I prepare for unexpected turbulence ahead. Part of my preparation had been memorizing the verses that God recalled to my mind on the plane.

When the wave hits, we work to survive, trying to stay above water, looking out for debris, rocks, and other objects that might cause injury. When my personal storm was raging, there were times when it was a matter of survival—mainly the survival of my faith. It was hard to believe a good God could let Joye suffer the way she did.

I remember sitting in her hospital room one day and crying more because of my fears and doubts than because of her condition. God reminded me of how David "recounted the goodness of God" in the Psalms. So for a couple of hours, I prayed and meditated on all the good things God had done for us—all the past spectacular answers to prayer, all the times God had intervened to spare us from pain. I concluded then that He is good! And the giant missing piece—the answer to the question "Why?"—had to be left totally in His hands. I couldn't understand it, but I could hang on.

After the storm passes, we wait for the water to subside. After Jack and I got back from overseas, even though God had done the initial healing, I experienced something that scared me. I found my emotions vacillating between tears at any moment and numbness. It was the numbness I hated most, because it spilled over into my time with God. I wasn't being lifted up with Him in my devotional times. I was just *blah.*

A friend suggested that my numbness might be an attack of Satan. Another friend felt that it was part of the scar tissue to protect the wound, and God would dissolve it in time. Frankly, I still don't know.

But I do know that it gradually disappeared. My heart began to soar as I studied the Word. My bubble of joy became more consistent. It just took time for the water to subside.

After the water subsides, we clean up the mess. That means getting rid of twisted conceptions about God and sifting through mutilated lessons we've learned that come to the surface again during the storm. In my life, there was a lot of debris that looked quite familiar! I had to ask myself over and over, *Carole, didn't you learn that last year, or ten years ago, or even twenty years ago? Do you have to keep learning things over and over?*

The answer is yes.

I used to think our learning was a steady upward growth—

relearning lessons, but at a higher level each time. In a sense this is true. If I am growing in the knowledge of Christ, I shouldn't be struggling with the same things year after year.

A friend's illustration helped me to comprehend the way we grow in discernment and understanding. He suggested that learning is like a camera. When the shutter opens to the light, we think, *Ah, I see it.* But then the shutter closes. A while later it opens once more but shuts soon thereafter.

Learning, or growth, is the process of making the shutter stay open a bit longer and of seeing a bit clearer each time. Instead of thinking, *Oh, I've finally seen the light. I'm sure I'll know how to deal with that problem forever*, perhaps we should learn the "lesson of the lens" and not condemn ourselves when we forget the truth for a time. Instead we should pray that the shutter will stay open a bit longer next time—that we will see deeper application and have clearer focus each time it opens.

You see, I knew about the "sacrifice of praise" and how we should offer it to God in every circumstance. I've written about it, spoken on it, and believe it with all my heart. But when I saw my sister's pain, the shutter of that lesson was very closed indeed. I could quote verses on being joyful in tribulation and wax eloquent on troubles bringing forth the gold in our lives. Thankfulness was one of those valuable items I had learned about long ago. But the application of it was almost nonexistent in those months of Joye's suffering. There was much debris I had to get rid of first. I had to give God my doubts, anger, and emotions before the shutter opened again for me. I trust that now I will see through the open lens of God's perspective for a longer period.

One night Jack and I were sitting by a roaring fire, talking of our growing responsibilities, of the problems of ones we count dear, and of seemingly insurmountable difficulties. I sighed and mused aloud, "It seems that the courses get more difficult as we get closer to graduation."

The truth of what I'd just thought out loud struck me. As we grow older, and nearer our departure into heaven, God knows we have much to learn in order to be ready. Sometimes it seems we must take a crash course—through pain, suffering, pressures—in order to be prepared for graduation and for meeting Him.

It had been some crash course for me! But instead of letting it drown me, God had dissipated the tidal wave. May I never forget the lessons learned by its approach.

## FOR REFLECTION

1. What are some tidal waves you've faced?
2. How does hope affect the tidal waves of life?
3. What is God asking you to "let"?

# CHAPTER THIRTEEN

# Leaks

Help Lord . . .
Help Lord . . .
Help Lord . . .

We call him Dr. Bob. Not only is he an outstanding medical doctor who hears about many people's aches, pains, and frustrations, he's also a warm and sympathetic Christian man. One time Jack and I were bending his ear about a deep tiredness we had been experiencing in recent weeks. He asked a few questions and listened intently. Then he began talking about how "emotional leaks" cause fatigue and drain a person's energy. Several times he used this term, but I let it pass, assuming I knew his meaning.

About the fourth time he used the phrase "emotional leak," I asked, "Dr. Bob, just what is your definition of an emotional leak?" He paused and then said something I didn't want to hear at all. He said, "Well, I guess an emotional leak is any area in which we are not fully trusting God."

Ouch.

As I was thinking about this statement later, it occurred to me to begin looking at all the little waves in my life to see if they were filling my boat with water. Was my problem the waves themselves, or was it my reaction to the waves? Were the pain and discomfort and tiredness I was experiencing caused by circumstances I couldn't control or by leaks—my lack of trust in the midst of those situations?

It was discouraging to realize a great part of my problem was the leaks. I would repair one only to have three others spurt open. Yet, in another way, it was encouraging. If the leaks were causing the dampness and discomfort, they were something I didn't have to put up with! The waves I couldn't do much about; the leaks could be repaired!

One Sunday afternoon I read the verse, "I will sing of the mercies of the Lord forever," but instead I cried most of the afternoon. There were two big waves tossing me about, but not much water would have entered my boat had it not been for my lack of trust during those two situations.

It wasn't so much the water splashing over the sides that was causing me pain, it was the water coming in through the cracks. Water can seep in through cracks, even on a quiet sea. Even in calm waters our boat will sink if it has a lot of internal ruptures. Water either buoys us up or drowns us, depending on what shape our boat is in. So the answer to the little waves and leaks is internal maintenance.

It takes more than just realizing that what I've been calling waves are, in actuality, leaks. I need God's help to stop the seepage. So what can I do to make my boat internally secure?

First of all, I must ask God for wisdom to discern whether the problem I am encountering is a wave or a leak—or in some cases both. I need to identify precisely the cause of the pain.

For instance, I may feel utterly drained from severe criticism—a wave I may or may not have caused. If it is a valid criticism, I need to take constructive action, to ask forgiveness and make amends. But let's suppose it's totally untrue and something I can't do anything about. That is a wave. However, if I am devastated by it, and unable to function, that is a leak. Why? Because it shows I am not trusting God fully to handle that situation. I am not trusting His love and sovereignty, His ability to "work things together for good," and His capacity to deal with the person who did the criticizing.

Have you ever felt that trusting God concerning someone else is harder than trusting God for yourself? I have. One thing that drains my emotional energy is seeing friends go through terrible problems that seem to have no end. I begin to feel that God is very slow in answering requests for them. Why does this drain my energy? Because in that situation I have given up believing that God will eventually work out the problem for that person's good. I begin to feel that the situation must be beyond hope. I don't acknowledge it consciously, but unconsciously that must be what I'm thinking or I wouldn't feel so drained.

I am drained emotionally when my schedule gets jammed with too many things. I seem to be juggling a dozen balls in the air and constantly dropping a few of them. One summer day, I sat in the parking lot of a shopping center and screamed. (I had the car windows closed, so no policeman checked me out.) It made me feel a little better, but not much.

A harried morning had been climaxed with a trip to the grocery store. In the checkout line, I found my checkbook was missing. Jack had been paying bills that morning and neglected to give the checkbook back to me. Leaving the grocery cart in the sanctuary of the dairy cooler, I rushed home, grabbed the checkbook, and hurried back to rescue my purchases. It was just past noon when I dared the hassle of crossing traffic to get to the small post office on the other side of the shopping center only to discover it was closed for lunch. It was at that point that I screamed.

The morning had been taken up with unworthy, inconsequential matters. It exasperated me and left me frustrated.

But wait! Hadn't I given the day to the Lord just that morning? Yes. Had He taken it? I had to believe so. Then why was I screaming in the parking lot? Obviously I wasn't relaxing in the fact that He was in control of my day. I wasn't believing that "there are enough hours in the day to do all God wants me to do" (a saying Jack reminds me of faithfully). Thus, my boat had sprung a leak.

Second, if a leak is an area in which I am not trusting God, then I simply have to learn to trust God more. How do I do that? As I reflected on this I realized how I had developed trust in Jack. If Jack, after we had just gotten married, had stayed out all night and come home with some wild and improbable story, I wouldn't have believed him. But today if he stayed out all night and told me that same story, I would believe him. Why? Because over the years Jack has proven to be a trustworthy person. It wasn't anything I did that developed that trust — except to live with him, observe him, and get to know his true character. So it is with God. We don't "crank up" faith. We simply get to know our God, who is faithful.

The third thing we must do is to wait for the Lord to strengthen us. We must go to Him daily with our specific list of leaks and ask Him to help us plug the openings, then leave those problems with Him. Oh, it's so important to wait *on* and *for* the Lord! Sometimes this means for a protracted time rather than just our daily devotional period.

One day God showed me the imperative need to wait. I wrote the following:

> I am numb. Movement swirls around me without my caring. The uncomfortable wetness at the bottom of my boat goes unnoticed. I know the roar of the storm is there, but I don't hear it. It's as if I am in the eye of the cyclone and the pressure has caused an eerie absence of sound. People are talking but not touching me with their words. All emotion has been drained from me.
>
> I am sitting here staring at nothing, waiting for feeling to flood again into my senses. I don't like this state, and I reflect on its causes: weeks filled with people, places, personalities, problems, pleasure, and pressures; needing to be "up" when I was "down"; going on reserve and using up my resources; not having time to soak in the Word or God's quiet and peace. They have been wonderful weeks really—seeing God working in situations and knowing His hand was supporting every facet of every day.
>
> And now all my energy—all feeling—has drained away. What will I do?
>
> I will wait.
>
> I will remember that "this too shall pass" and not allow myself to believe it is interminable.
>
> I will wait and remember that in God's time He will give some hours of quiet and peace. Until such a time comes, He will give me the ability to absorb His quiet in the midst of activity and pressure.
>
> I will wait, recalling that the Spirit of Him who raised Christ from the dead will give life to my mortal body through His Spirit who indwells me (see Romans 8:11).

I will wait, and as I wait, God will renew my strength and I will soar above my day—lifted above even the ability or inability to feel, to touch, to sense—and learn to walk and run without fainting, but only in His strength.

I will wait, realizing that even this numbness is a form of rest to my spirit, coming straight from the hand of God. I will wait, realizing, too, that when our bodies are physically tired, we need extra physical rest. But when our emotions, our spirits, our minds are tired, we need to "consider him that endured such contradiction of sinners against himself, lest ye be wearied and faint in your *minds*" (Hebrews 12:3, KJV, emphasis added). The answer to emotional weariness lies in considering Jesus.

Help me, Lord, to consider You—really!

In order to wait on the Lord, we must "come apart." The necessity for this is absolute. It has been said that if you don't come apart, you will come apart!

It was a brilliant blue-sky summer morning in Colorado, and I was in my favorite quiet-time spot—our tiny porch off our bedroom, which overlooks the mountains. The Lord and I were having a delightful time together that was food and life to my heart after a period of spiritual famine. I was praying and meditating on Psalm 143:8: "Let the morning bring me word of your unfailing love, for I have put my trust in you. Show me the way I should go, for to you I lift up my soul." I was truly hearing God's lovingkindness that morning.

"Why is it, Lord," I asked, "that my times with You are not always so refreshing? Why is it that at times Your voice is so silent or so far away?"

"Because you don't come apart," He answered to my heart.

"But how can I come apart always, Father? When our house is full of guests, when I'm on a jam-packed ministry trip, when my schedule is full of urgent considerations, when—"

I stopped talking as God flashed thought remembrances into my mind. In the Bible, Mary allowed another person to shoulder responsibilities so that she could sit at Jesus' feet and hear Him. John Wesley's mother couldn't leave her many children, so she taught them not to disturb her when she had her apron over her head. A friend of mine trades a morning a week of child care with another busy mother so she can go to a park or library to spend extended time with God.

I hear God best on the quiet days—when I can get up early and not feel the pressures of a busy day demanding my time and attention. But how many days like that do any of us actually have?

If I'm really going to hear Him in the morning of my soul, it's going to take thought, planning, discipline, time, and asking Him for creative ideas. But do it I must. If I have to slip away from my company to go to a nearby park for an hour or so, I should do it. If I have to ask for an hour or two alone when on a trip, I must ask.

I must have inner quietness. I must ask God for the ability to be tranquil, to listen, to be still inside, even when the world is falling apart outside.

The fourth thing I must do to make my boat secure is to have the leaks repaired by God. This can be no halfhearted attempt, no game I play to delude myself. Some leaks are so small that I may be tempted to ignore them or too lazy to deal with them. They may not swamp my boat, but they will most surely hinder my progress.

We know that worry is a lack of trust, and therefore sin. We call it "concern" and live with it for years. *Any* lack of trust in God is sin. I need to call it just that. So an emotional leak in my life is sin and must not be tolerated!

Psalm 34 is a tremendous song of deliverance. David talks about God delivering him from fear, poverty or want, trouble, a broken heart, a crushed spirit, afflictions, and danger. It would seem that this list covers just about every possible wave in life. The secret of God's deliverance from these things is found in verses 4-6: "I sought the Lord . . . Those who look . . . This poor man called."

God will deliver us as we ask, as we wait, and as we seek Him. But we have to mean business.

Do you remember the story of Jacob when he wrestled all night with the angel of the Lord? Jacob was determined! He meant business when he said, "I will not let you go unless you bless me" (Genesis 32:26).

There have been times in my life when I have wrestled, as it were, with God. I was desperate to get rid of a burden, release a worry, regain strength and joy—desperate enough to go to the Lord for however long was necessary and cry, "Lord, You promised, and I need You. I need Your strength for my weakness, Your peace for my turbulent heart, Your grace to help me soar, Your release for this burden, Your forgiveness for this failure. I will not leave this place until You give me what I know You want me to have."

And then I wait. God has never failed to meet me. Oh, it is not always a hundred-pound sack of His grace that He delivers to my door. Sometimes it is only a quiet whisper, "All is well—go forward and see."

The leaks in my life can and must and will be plugged as I . . .

⑥ ask God to identify the leaks
⑥ take time to know Him as the faithful One
⑥ wait for Him to give me the ability to truly trust Him for every drain in my life
⑥ remain committed to stopping those leaks

When the leaks have been stopped, my boat will ride high on the water, defying the waves, and I will know without a doubt that Christ is truly Lord of my rocking boat.

### FOR REFLECTION
1. What are some of the "leaks" in your life?
2. How can you willingly take your hand away from those leaks and trust God to take care of them?
3. How easy is it for you to "come apart" to fellowship with God? What can you do to come apart more often?

# WHO THEN IS THIS?

*SUDDENLY, THE STORM STILLS. THE DISCIPLES LOOK AT THE MIRROR calmness of the sea, which moments before had been wild and tormented. Amazement shines from eyes that are wide with fear and wonder as they whisper together, "Who then is this that even the waves and the wind obey him?"*

*God delights to bring us through the storms! Often we exclaim, "I perish, for problems far too big for me to solve are piled higher than my head" (Psalm 40:12, TLB). We must remember at that moment, "O Lord my God, many and many a time you have done great miracles for us, and we are ever in your thoughts. Who else can do such glorious things? No one else can be compared with You. There isn't time to tell of all Your wonderful deeds" (Psalm 40:5, TLB).*

*In the midst of our storms, we need to declare, "O my soul, why be so gloomy and discouraged? Trust in God! I shall again praise Him for His wondrous help; He will make me smile again" (Psalm 43:5, TLB).*

*The storms are necessary to teach us, but the sunshine is also His gift to us. We may be so wet from the storm that we are not aware of the sun emerging through the clouds. We don't even see the rays, let alone feel their warmth on our faces or pause to thank the Father for their presence.*

*Life is full of small and large problems and pains—the waves and the* leaks. But God is in the business of giving moments of sunlight, warmth, and joy during the storms as well as speaking a final "Peace" to them. Unless we learn to experience the moments of brightness and remember that God will bring an end to the turbulence, we will live in defeat, without joy.

In the hush that followed the tidal wave in my life, I was able to look clearly at its lessons and allow them to sink deeply into my life. Perhaps in the ferocity of the larger gales of life, we have to wait for the storm to be stilled before we comprehend the lessons. Hebrews 12:11 reminds us that "no discipline seems pleasant at the time, but painful. Later on, however, it produces a harvest of righteousness and peace for those who have been trained by it." I don't believe that all storms fall into the category of discipline from God, but I do believe that afterwards, when they bring righteousness and peace, then we understand something of what has happened to us.

However, if we can't see the fleeting joys and delights during the smaller storms of life, we may dwell in poverty surrounded by the riches of God's grace. My prayer is that as we consider the brief glimpses of sunshine, as well as the great quiet at the end of the storm, our eyes might be focused on the delights God gives us instead of the dilemmas on which we often fix our minds. In the Psalms, David "recounted the goodness of God" to bring happiness to his heart. So let's center our thoughts on the joys of life God showers on those who look for His delights.

# CHAPTER FOURTEEN

# Soaring

Help Lord . . .
Help Lord . . .
Help Lord . . .

I often have the opportunity to drive in and out of The Navigators Conference Center at Glen Eyrie in Colorado Springs. Glen Eyrie means "Valley of the Eagles," and there is a large eagle's nest up on the side of a cliff. Every so often the eagles come back, repair the nest, and use it for their young. One spring we were excited to discover them fixing the nest. In time, we observed an eaglet's head appearing above the twisted branches. The next month we saw the eaglet on the edge of the nest, stretching and flapping its wings. For many days the eaglet exercised, until at last it took flight and soared above the earth.

I long to soar like that eagle. But again I must ask, "Yes, Lord, but how?"

God gave me some insight on this from Isaiah 40:28-31. Isaiah wrote,

Do you not know? Have you not heard?
The everlasting God, the Lord, the creator of the ends of
the earth
Does not become weary or tired.
His understanding is inscrutable. He gives strength to the
weary,

And to him who lacks might he increases power.
Though youths grow weary and tired,
And vigorous young men stumble badly,
Yet those who wait for the Lord will gain new strength;
They will mount up with wings like eagles,
They will run and not get tired,
They will walk and not become weary. (NASB)

One of the most comforting parts of this passage, and a great encouragement in itself, is to know that God understands. "His understanding is inscrutable." I love that! *Inscrutable* means "unfathomable, that which cannot be easily understood, incomprehensible, beyond interpretation." And so it is. He understands when people discourage me with their decisions, attitudes, demands, and problems. He understands and is able to give me strength when I'm weary (and oh, I get so weary). He will even increase my power.

The second principle to comprehend is that God wants us to mount up with wings like eagles—to see people and problems from His point of view, to have His perspective on the finite matters we trudge through each day. He wants us to soar, to be lifted up close to the Son, warmed by His presence and drawn close to His heart where we can feel Him.

I am such a feeling-oriented person that it's not enough for me to know the truths of God in my head. In order to soar, I must also *feel* His truths in my heart.

The secret of soaring is found in Isaiah 40:31. It is engraved in the words, "Wait on the Lord." The word *wait* in Hebrew means to "entwine my heart around." As I wait on the Lord through His Word, the truths He reveals will help me soar.

I find that I need my intake valves wide open if I want to fly high! They are the most important part of my soaring mechanism and are vital for obtaining the power to soar with God. One valve that can easily get clogged is *hearing* the Word of God. As we listen (church, radio, other Christians) we need to hear with our hearts in order to let the Holy Spirit apply the words as He will.

Another valve that gets clogged is our *reading* valve. God's small but insistent voice should be clearly heard as we thoughtfully and consistently read His Word.

A great piece of dirt often blocks the valve called *study*—that is, personal, creative, individual study apart from preparing a Sunday school lesson or devotional talk.

*Memorizing* the Word is another vital means of intake.

The fifth valve operates only if the first four are wide open. This valve is *meditating* not only on what we've memorized but on what we've heard, read, and studied.

Hearing the Word can also mean asking the right questions of other Christians and listening to what others have to say. Reading and study are limited to a particular time for our devotions or those hours regularly reserved for prolonged study and time with God.

Memorizing Scripture buys up many otherwise wasted, useless moments of our lives and can be sandwiched in splinters of time. Meditation—or mental Bible study with application—should be going on whenever our minds are not occupied with other concerns.

If our intake of God's Word is functioning at full capacity, then we should be soaring, entwining our hearts about the heart of God. But what if we aren't? What if we're doing all these things yet we're crashing with a thud? It's possible.

Two things have helped me immeasurably.

First, I pray often that God will give me an *insatiable hunger for Himself and His Word*—a thirst for righteousness. I pray that He will draw me to Himself and give me an increasing desire to know Him and have a greater love for Him, each day.

Second, I pray for an *expectant heart*. I ask the Lord to help me soar, to find delight in His Word.

When you are depending on God for the desire to really know Him, and your intake valves are wide open, unblocked by self or sin, you *will* soar. To soar is to experience delight when you see something in God's Word that makes you want to jump up, clap your hands, and exclaim, "Wow! Just look at that!"

Soaring is being able to see your problems as God sees them—in the light of all eternity. It is experiencing grace in the form of patience or joy or strength, or whatever you need at that particular moment, a grace which you know is not in you but from Him.

For instance, a number of situations in my life leave me feeling totally inadequate. One time, as I was praying about a particularly overwhelming group of people I was to speak to, I said to the Lord, "What have You gotten me into this time?" He spoke firmly to my heart, "Nothing *I* can't handle, my child."

Soon after that, as I was reading the story of Elisha in 2 Kings 4, God really made me soar. The widow who had previously befriended Elisha cried to him that her boys were about to be sold into slavery to pay her dead husband's creditors. Elisha asked how he could help and then said, "Tell me, what do you have in your house?" "Your servant has nothing there at all," she said, "except a little oil" (2 Kings 4:2).

You may remember that God, through Elisha, multiplied that bit of oil so that the woman paid all her debts and lived on the proceeds from the rest.

God said to me, "Carole, what do you have in your house?" and I said, "Nothing! Except this little message to present that You have helped me prepare." He replied, "Give it to Me and I'll multiply it."

I wanted to stand up and shout! It wasn't my feeble message that was going to do anything—it was the God of the message who would accomplish what He willed!

Many times we say, "Oh, I can't do anything," but God says, "What do you have in your house?" We reply, "Nothing, only an ability to tell a story, or a sense of humor, or the ability to pray, or to bake bread." God's response is always, "Give it to Me and I'll multiply it."

The times of discovering delights in God's Word are soaring times. They get my mind off the problems and onto the Problem Solver. And as He becomes my focus, He gives me added strength to "walk and not become weary" and to "run and not get tired" (Isaiah 40:31).

He does it all, you know. He gives us the desire to soar, the wings with which to do it, the discipline to exercise those wings, and the knowledge to use them.

While that eaglet we watched couldn't fly right away at first, it was born with wings that would eventually enable it to soar far above the earth. Now, an eagle isn't always soaring. She has to come down to rest and eat and tend to her housekeeping duties and the raising of her children. But even while she's doing the "dailies," I suspect that with a part of her soul (if eagles have souls!) she is far above the world, soaring on the currents of the winds. She's remembering what it's like to be way up above her responsibilities and circumstances.

So it is with me. I can't soar all the time, but my heart's longing is to soar with God by delighting in His Word daily, and then always keep in my mind His perspective on the world when I am again involved with the necessities of life.

When we are spiritually born into God's kingdom by receiving Christ into our lives, we are born with "spiritual wings" to soar with God. How sad it is that some of us proceed to fold our wings under us and let them atrophy. We never use them. Others allow so many weights to accumulate that they can't rise above the ground.

I don't want my wings to atrophy and become useless. Oh yes, there are times when I seem to soar only two feet above the ground. At other times my wings seem to be brushing the rocks and dragging in the dirt. But I'm learning to stretch my wings, catch the currents of God's Spirit, and soar!

### FOR REFLECTION

1. Do you long to soar? Ask God to give you a hunger for Him and His Word. Ask also for an expectant heart as you await the results.
2. What do you have in your house? How can you give those things to God for Him to multiply?
3. In what kind of shape are your "wings?" How can you exercise them this week?

# CHAPTER FIFTEEN

# The God of Sunshine

Help Lord . . .
Help Lord . . .
Help Lord . . .

In her book *Discovering the Joy of Obedience*, Hope MacDonald tells of a friend in Brazil who lived in a tiny three-room house with thirteen children and two other adults. She was thirty-seven, looking seventy, when Hope had the privilege of introducing her to Christ. Hope spent a year helping her in her Christian life.

> As I watched Dona Jesse grow in the love and knowledge of the Lord, I saw a transformation take place in her life that could only come from God. Her face became alive with the joy of the Lord. A twinkle was added to her eyes, and she had an insatiable hunger to learn all she could about God's Word.
>
> A year later when I entered the back door of Dona Jesse's little house, I sensed something was different. She met me with a weary look of exhaustion and told me what had happened. Six days earlier her sister from the north had moved in with her. With her came her ten children, and they all had terrible cases of trench mouth. As a result, over half of Dona Jesse's thirteen children had come down with it too. The beds in the three stuffy rooms were filled

with sick children. All had burning fevers and mouths swollen with infected sores. As I looked at the tired, worn woman in front of me, I was filled with overwhelming sadness. Twenty-seven people were living in that house—most of them terribly sick. She had meals to prepare three times a day on the small woodburning stove, and endless demands required her attention.

I said quietly, "Dona Jesse, how are you doing in the midst of all this?" And as long as I live, I will never forget her response. Her face suddenly broke out in a radiant smile, and she said, "Right here, in my heart, everything is full of peace. I get up in the morning at 4:30 before anyone else is awake. I come out here and sit at the table and read my Bible and pray, and I thank God for all his many blessings to me!" As I looked around at the hopelessness of her situation, I couldn't see even one blessing. Yet she had a whole list![1]

Dona Jesse had the inner joy that Jesus came to give us in the midst of every situation of life. This joy has nothing to do with outward circumstances or other people. It comes only from within—constantly . . . always . . . continually.

We must keep our eyes on the Savior and not the storms (see Hebrews 12:2). We must ask God for the ability to feel His presence going into, at the very height of, and coming out of the tempests (see Isaiah 41:10). And when we can't feel Him, we must cling to His promises until the feeling comes.

As we ask, "Yes, but how?" a primary step is to look for the unique, the lovely, and the humorous—those things that are of "good report" (see Philippians 4:8). We must ask ourselves, "What can I find in this day, this situation, this moment to be glad and thankful for?" Some people are more naturally optimistic than others, but when more of God's grace is needed, more of God's grace will be received.

We may have to pray for awareness. I inherited my mother's optimistic nature but not her ability to find something to laugh about even in difficult situations. I have to pray to be able to see and enjoy God's delights.

Another great factor in developing a joyful heart is to recount

the goodness of God. How long has it been since you've deliberately sat down to think about His goodness? How many weeks have
gone by in which you were not aware of the sunset, the deep blue
of the sky, the fragrance of a lilac bush, or a child's laughter?

I'm wondering how often we take the time to savor such
moments of our lives. It seems to me that a great deal of quality
thinking time in my life is given over to problems rather than concentrating on the delights of life.

God tells us that we are what we think about (see Proverbs
23:7), and it follows that our attitudes about life will be determined
by what our thoughts dwell upon. If we practice thinking about what
is good and beautiful (Philippians 4:8), our days will be more delightful and joyous. I'm not saying it's easy, especially for those who tend
to be negative thinkers. But God never gives us a command without
giving us the ability in the Holy Spirit to obey it. So it is possible!

I've given some thinking time to the delight of love in my life.
At the top of my list for praise and thanksgiving is the delight of
having a caring husband.

I went out into the backyard one night, the sky almost black
in the early evening darkness of late November, and turned on
our new gas barbecue. A bit unfamiliar with its workings, I failed
to lift the hood, and some trapped gas exploded with a flash of fire
and a loud *bang*! A tongue of flame hit my hand as I yelped and
jerked away. I knew immediately that I was more scared than hurt.

Jack, about to change his clothes after jogging, had heard the
bang and my scream. Concern written all over his startled white face,
he appeared in the porch doorway, wearing only his sweat pants.

"Honey, are you all right?" he asked.

After I reassured him, he examined my hand (only slightly
red, with scorched-off hair) and the barbecue before returning to
his dressing.

I prayed then, "Oh, Father. What a joy and a delight—what a
privilege and blessing—to have a husband so caring, so loving, so
immediately there. How often Jack has dropped things important
to him in order to minister to my needs. Thank you for the delight
of having loved ones who care."

Love of husband, love of friends, love of children. What precious gifts from God.

My sister, Joye, who kept a record of incidents in her children's lives, wrote the following:

> Several operations and a skin condition left me with a large scar about two inches wide from my chin to the hollow of my throat. This occurred at puberty, and boys and girls made me more conscious of it as they looked at me with expressions of horror and exclaimed how ghastly it looked. It took me years to overcome the habit of keeping my head down and shoulders slumped to try to hide that scar.
>
> I married and had a boy and then a girl. My daughter was about seven when I found some cover-up makeup and was attempting to make my scar as inconspicuous as possible. Melody came into the room at the time and asked what I was doing. I replied that I was trying to cover up my hideous-looking scar. She looked horrified. "Oh, Mommie, don't do that! I just love your scar. I think it's just bea-u-ti-ful!" she exclaimed.
>
> I couldn't believe my ears. I looked at her in amazement. Her eyes shone with sincerity and love as she touched my scar tenderly. I hugged her close as I thought, *Truly, beauty is in the eye of the beholder.*

One of the pleasures of children is the fun and imagination they bring into our lives. Each age is filled with unique and humorous things they say and do. A dear friend of mine was listening to her four-year-old son praying. He said, "Thank you for the chickens that give us eggs. And thank you for the cows that give us milk. And thank you for the camels that give us soup!"

The enjoyment of children is experienced in moments picked one at a time and then bunched together to inhale the fragrance of memory. So often we let the moments, as well as the memories, wilt and die, rather than placing them under our remembrance glass, setting them on the mantel of our minds, and enjoying them frequently. God really does give us "all things to enjoy."

The key to inner joy is wrapped up in God Himself. Knowing Him intimately gave Dona Jesse the ability to list her blessings during chaos in her life. Focusing on the Savior ensures our ability to be aware of the sunbeams all around us. He is the Lord of delights and of love. And it isn't only the kind of love that children, husband, and friends shower upon us. He *personally* extends His love to us. His love accepts us and is constantly offered.

One morning I wrote:

> Her thoughts said, "Lord, as I was dressing this morning I noticed all the little scars, bumps, and blemishes that have developed through the years. The verse that a sacrifice to You had to be unblemished made me ponder the fact that I could never be a worthy sacrifice."
>
> The Lord said, "I see you unblemished, dear child. The blemishes on your soul—the scars and marks—are much greater than on your body and would make you an unacceptable sacrifice. But I see your soul as perfect, too."
>
> Then she remembered the Word of the Lord that said, "And you, who once were estranged and hostile in mind, doing evil deeds, he has now reconciled in his body of flesh by his death, in order to present you holy, blameless, and irreproachable before him." (Colossians 1:21-22, RSV)

This truth alone should fill us with wonder and joy! God has showered the riches of His grace upon us—more than we will ever be able to comprehend. Let's soak them in, savoring carefully God's delights as He gives them to us one by one.

### FOR REFLECTION

1. What can you find in this day, this situation, this moment to be glad and thankful for?
2. Memorize Philippians 4:8. Meditate on it and practice it each day.

# CHAPTER SIXTEEN

# The God of Delights

Help Lord . . .
Help Lord . . .
Help Lord . . .

The address alone would have sold us on the house! When God opened the way to purchase it, we were delighted because the house was on Serendipity Circle! According to *Webster's Dictionary*, *serendipity* means "an apparent aptitude for making fortunate discoveries accidentally." But with God, nothing is accidental, so to me *serendipity* means "unexpected but planned of God."

God has prepared such delights around every corner, but we often don't see them. In this chapter, I'd like to consider a few of God's delights so that we may begin to be aware of the many He has stored up for us to enjoy.

### The Delight of Laughter

Our God, who created man after His own image, has given us a "funny bone." You will not find laughter among the list of spiritual gifts, but some people do not think the list is exhaustive. If not, perhaps the gift of laughter would be next on the roster. But whether or not it is a spiritual gift, it certainly is a blessing to us.

Laughter lightens our sometimes heavy loads. It helps the sunshine break through a rather dark internal day. According to Proverbs 17:22, it "does good like a medicine." The literal truth of

this has been verified in medicine today. Laughter can be an anti-
dote to stress-related diseases. Some physicians claim that 90
percent of illnesses are stress related.

I heard one eminent psychiatrist say that you should not marry
a person who doesn't have the ability to laugh, including the ability to laugh at himself. Most people who have a good sense of
humor are able to do that.

Some see humor in situations where others can't, and it makes
life for everyone a bit easier. Joye was like that. She loved to laugh.
There were times when she could see humor in a situation that no
one else thought was funny. Her laughter, which ran up and down
the scale before she inhaled with a sound somewhere between a
note and a shriek, would draw us all into her merriment.

She laughed often. She could extract humor from ordinary situations, and in the retelling of an otherwise routine incident, have
her audience giggling along with her. She loved a good story and
milked it for all it was worth. We loved her for it.

I wonder how many times you've prayed for the ability to
laugh, to see the humor in situations, to have a "merry heart." It
could be a valuable request to put on your prayer list.

In Forest Lawn cemetery in California, life-sized figures of a
small boy and girl and a furry puppy stand looking up at the
Founders Creed, making you want to read the words carved in
stone. One sentence I remember especially. It says, "Most of all I
believe in a Christ who smiles and loves you and me."

I like that! "A Christ who smiles and loves." Of course He
does. In a movie about Jesus, based on the Gospel of Luke, Christ
laughed out loud several times. I'm sure He did when He walked
on earth, and He does now. In the course of a day, I sometimes
shake my head and think, "Oh, Lord, You must be having a good
laugh over that one!" And I chuckle, too. Aren't you glad for the
unexpected laughter and delights that lie around every corner of
life? May God give us the ability to laugh!

### The Delight of My Special Name
"It is absolutely amazing to me," my friend said excitedly, "how
much my five-year-old daughter has changed since I stopped thinking of her as 'my stubborn child.' A few weeks ago, God spoke to

me about changing the negative name I had given her in my thoughts to a positive one. So I began thinking of her as 'my sunshine child.' I started to compliment her on her bright smile and happy attitude. You wouldn't believe how she's changed!"

Psychologists have talked about self-fulfilling prophecies and have warned of the danger of labeling others or ourselves in a negative way. Dr. James Dobson's "no-knock" policy was a recent challenge to me. It's a determination — like a vow — that I will not criticize or cut down anyone, including myself. I had gotten into the habit of calling myself "old dumb Carole" when I did something rather stupid. Dobson's "no-knock" rule helped me become aware of what I was doing.

However, I didn't realize how often I mentally labeled others in my mind. I called them an "on-time-person" or "always-late-person" or "spacey one" or "businesslike" or whatever.

Then I saw with clarity that it was God who first came up with the "no-knock" policy and went one step further. God calls His children by unique, complimentary names. God always looks for and remembers the best about us and gives us a name to suit what He sees in us.

God called Daniel a "man of high esteem" (Daniel 10:11). The Son of God complimented and called attention to the good in Daniel. I noticed that but felt, because Daniel seemed to be such an exemplary character, that he had earned it somehow.

Sarai was a different matter! Sarai was cruel to Hagar, devious with Abraham, and lied to an angel! Nevertheless, God overlooked all of those negative characteristics and called her a "holy woman of God" (see 1 Peter 3:5-6).

David was a murderer, an adulterer, and who knows what else, but God called him a "man after God's own heart."

The climax for me was to find in Revelation 2:17 that God calls us all by a secret special name. And we may be sure that new name, as an adopted and beloved child of His, is a good name. I wonder what mine is!

### The Delight of God's Concern
I hadn't thought of it in a long time, but when I wasn't able to get to sleep one night I began reflecting on the ways of God in my life.

I recalled in graphic detail the first time God proved Himself to me. As I reflected, I was awed by the multitude of happenings God had to arrange to accomplish what He did.

I couldn't have been more than eight years old, possibly not even that, but I was having my first deep struggle of faith. I don't remember what set it off, but doubts and questions had been raging in my mind for several days. "Have I been told a fairy tale? Is there really a God who looks over the world and cares about me? Does He exist? How can a person really know that He is there?"

I told no one of my struggle, but it seethed inside me until it surfaced one night in a small town in Michigan. We were visiting a favorite aunt and uncle, and I was put to bed in an upstairs room located under the eaves. The roof sloped steeply and overhung the small window. It was there that my struggle formed and took shape. It was there that I challenged God to prove to me that He existed. The challenge was not one of shaking my fist at God and demanding, "Prove yourself to me." Rather, born of desperation, it was a cry. "Oh, Lord, I want to believe in You. I need desperately to know that You are there. Please show Yourself to me."

I didn't feel I could ask for a vision or a voice from heaven. So, in my immature, nonthinking way, I blurted out, "Oh, God, just prove to me that You are there by—by—by waking me up with the moon shining in the window."

Then I went to sleep.

Silly girl, never thinking that God would have to bend the moon many degrees, or even take it out of the sky to make it shine in that window way back under the eaves. Never thinking that there might not even be a moon that evening. Never thinking. Period.

But God was thinking, and preparing.

First He sent some other guests to my aunt's that night. This meant that the bed I was in was needed for an adult, so I was moved to the davenport in the living room, without even waking up.

Second, God arranged for my aunt and uncle to have a house with a round window located on a landing going to the second floor. He also had my aunt locate the furniture so that the davenport was in exactly the right spot.

Third, He created a clear sky and full moon.

Sometime that night, I was awakened as though a gentle hand

had touched my shoulder. And there, framed perfectly in that port-hole window, was a full moon beaming like a spotlight.

I got out of bed, fell to my knees, and cried for joy. "Lord," I said, "I promise You I will never again doubt that You exist. Thank You."

And I never have. Oh, I've had my share of doubts that He could use me, that He had a plan for me, even doubts about His character. But never doubts that He exists. The God of all detail had proven to me on that desperate night that He is there and He is not silent.

### The Delight of God's Care
One morning, as I was thinking about the love and care of God, I read this story:

> A missionary found herself without means, among a hea-then people, far from any source of supplies. In her distress she claimed the promise of God that he would supply her need. She was also in poor health. From a businessman in another part of the country came several large boxes of Scotch oatmeal. She already had several cans of condensed milk, so with these two commodities, she was obliged to sustain life for four long weeks. As time went on, it seemed to agree with her better; and by the time the four weeks had passed, she felt in excellent health. In relating the experience some time later to a company of people, which included a physician, she was asked more particularly of the nature of her former illness. The physician said, "The Lord heard your prayer and supplied your need more truly than you realize. For the sickness from which you were suffering, we physicians prescribe a four weeks' diet of nothing but oatmeal gruel for our patients. The Lord pre-scribed it for you, and saw to it that was all you took. It was the proper remedy."[1]

God's understanding truly is inscrutable! He demonstrates that fact in arranging the details of life so that a small child can know He exists and in providing the perfect diet for an ill missionary. It is very evident in the Scriptures as well.

Jack and I have only been to Israel once, very briefly, and the parts we saw where the land had not been cultivated were rocky, dry, and brown. I was therefore interested in the account of Christ feeding the five thousand (probably more like eighteen or twenty thousand because the miracle doesn't record how many women and children accompanied those five thousand men). In recounting that story, three of the Gospels take a moment to describe that there was grass there (see Matthew 14:19; Mark 6:39; John 6:10, KJV). In fact, in John it says, "There was much grass in the place."

God never wastes words. Therefore there must be a reason that the Holy Spirit led John to tell us about the condition of the hillside.

Five thousand men, plus women and children, had followed Christ to the mountain where He was meeting with His disciples. His concern was to feed that crowd. Probably many of the little ones were becoming weak, and all were very hungry. Christ was looking out for their needs. But that isn't all!

He was also concerned for their comfort. He chose a place—and it was important enough to record for all history—for them to sit down where there was "much grass."

Personally, I think God had been preparing that hillside for months. The Creator of the universe had seen to it that life-giving rains had brought greenness to that slope, and the sun had helped to make the grass thick and lush. He had prepared it for their comfort as they listened.

God's eye is always toward us! He is always looking out for our needs—even the "extras," the comforts of life—if they are best for us. "In the morning he thinks of the day before you are astir! He is waiting long before you are awake. His anticipations are along all the way of life before you."[2] Sometimes He knows we need the uncomfortable rocks to make us "endurers," to toughen us against the winds of adversity. But when He knows the comfort is for our good, He desires to delight us with "much grass."

### The Delight of Our Inheritance

Six weeks into our trip overseas, Jack and I found ourselves in a delightful village high above a valley in Switzerland. On a tiny balcony off our hotel room I wrote:

I am sitting by a window viewing a panorama of the Alps—sun and shadow on snowcapped peaks and rugged bare rocks, lush green forests and a fertile valley below. The Matterhorn peeks above a band of white clouds, its height dwarfing the other majestic peaks. Breathtaking beauty.

And yet—God whispers—"only a foretaste." Last night in a delightful French-Swiss restaurant, we ate delicious beef fondue with savory sauces. As it cooked at our table, delicious smells wafted from the bubbling pot— a foretaste of what we enjoyed a moment later.

As magnificent a view as the world can provide is before me. Still, it is just a foretaste—a scent of the real thing. Heaven is the real thing.

Thank you, Lord, that Mom and Dad and Joye are experiencing at this moment the real thing!

The closer I get to going to heaven, the more I delight in thinking about what lies ahead. We are given only a scant description of that place, limited I am sure by the capability of our finite minds to picture what is infinite and beyond our most expansive dreams. But it's fun to imagine some of the delights of our future. Some things I'm very sure of; others are "I'll-just-betcha" dreams.

Among the things I am sure of are these: We are going to be more alive, more alert, more vitally *there* than here. "Now we see but a poor reflection as in a mirror; then we shall see face to face" (1 Corinthians 13:12). The contrast will be like deepest shadow and brilliant sunlight—and this earth is the shadow. I used to think of heaven as a shadowy, vague place where we'd all float around wondering what to do. Not any more! This earth, as we look back on it, will be the vague place. Instead of the five senses we have now, I think we will have six or seven or more—to better experience being vitally, joyfully alive to the wonder that will surround us. Every sense we have now will be working at 100 percent capacity to enable us to enjoy the beauty, the sounds, the smell, the touch, and the taste of heaven.

In Mark 4:35 we read, "When evening came, he said to his disciples, 'Let us go over to the other side.'" When the evening of our life comes, Christ will speak those words to us: "Let us go over to the other side." We may be sure He will accompany us on that breathtaking journey.

The son asked, What is death?

His Savior answered, I will come again and receive you unto myself; that where I am, there ye may be also.

The son repeated those peaceful words, *I will receive you unto myself . . .* and he wondered that men had given so harsh a name to anything so gentle as that which those words signified.  They seemed melodious to him, each word like the pure note of a bell. And they were, he thought, as full of life as a flower in the sunshine is full of light.[3]

God's delights are everywhere! Sometimes in the storms of our lives there doesn't seem to be any break in the dark, threatening clouds. But in other instances, we don't see the sunshine because we're not willing to look. It takes too much effort to live above the storm. We need to pray constantly with the psalmist, "Open my eyes that I may see" (Psalm 119:18).

May we see Him always — each moment, each day — through the storms and the sunshine until at last we meet Him face-to-face.

*Lord, Thank You for the waves—the tidal waves and all the little waves too. I am so grateful that all have taught me more of You, Your faithfulness, Your care, Your love. Thank You for keeping me safe, even in the midst of the wild turbulence. And then, thank You for the "Peace, be still"s that You have spoken in my life, for bringing me through the storms, for plugging the leaks, and for bringing me into the delights of Your sunshine. Help me to be aware, increasingly, of that sunshine. Even when I'm getting wet, help me to know that Your presence alone brings sunshine.*

*And when You choose to bring me safely to the shore of Your final delight—heaven and Your presence forever—help me to have lived this life of storm and sunshine in a way that pleases You. Amen.*

**FOR REFLECTION**

1. Think about your special name. What do you think it might be? What can you do to live up to it?
2. How would calling others by their special names change how you view them? Think of special names for those you're closest to or those with whom you have conflict. Practice using these names.
3. What are some ways you could focus on God's delights—even if you're "getting wet"?

Help Lord . . .

Help Lord . . .

Help Lord . . .

PART THREE

# Filled to Overflowing

. . . I'm Sinking

# CHAPTER SEVENTEEN

# Looking to Jesus

Help Lord . . .
Help Lord . . .
Help Lord . . .

The hair dryer clicked off. Voices that had been blurred by the hum of the dryer now focused sharply. A ripple of laughter eddied around me.

I found myself unavoidably tuning in on a discussion about what should be done in case of nuclear attack. Three women were agreeing that to try to flee the city before it was demolished would be futile. But what should they do?

Most people in Colorado Springs are aware that in the event of a nuclear attack, we would be leveled by the missiles aimed at Cheyenne Mountain. For beneath Cheyenne Mountain, which can be seen from anywhere in the city, are seven miles of tunnels housing NORAD—the North American Air Defense Command.

One woman said, "Well, I hope when it comes, I'll be in bed! I'd rather die in bed, especially if I'm in bed with someone I love." The others smiled and agreed that would be a good idea.

Another woman, who had obviously had to diet all her life, contributed this gem: "Well, I'm going to keep a giant hot-fudge sundae in my freezer, and when the alarm sounds, I'm going to rush to the refrigerator and eat it—and everything else in sight."

Everyone laughed. But the laughter was bordered by fear. And

I noticed that these women were not saying *if* a nuclear attack comes but *when* it comes, as if the future menaced them with inevitable doom.

I wanted to come from under the dryer to give each lady a hug and say, "You know, there's Someone who holds the fate of the world in His hands. He promised us, 'Though the earth be removed and the mountains carried into the sea, I am in your midst.' His name is Jesus."

How often our focus is shown in casual conversation. Our thinking, our mindset, is disclosed by nearly everything we do and say. Our attitudes reveal our focus. The conversation of those women in the beauty shop indicated their fear, frustration, and anxiety.

What a contrast to the outlook of Elisabeth Elliot, who returned to the dangerous jungles of Ecuador to reach out to the tribe of Indians who had brutally murdered her husband and four other missionaries. Elisabeth and her four-year-old daughter, Valerie, went back to a section of jungle notorious for its poisonous snakes. Just imagine your four-year-old walking around barefoot in such a place! Yet Elisabeth wrote from that jungle, "God has delivered me from *all* fear."

Psalm 34:4 promises, "I sought the LORD, and He answered me, and delivered me from all my fears" (NASB). Elisabeth's focus on God enabled her to have a courageous, fearless attitude.

Our focus is revealed by our attitude about life in general. But I'm finding that my focus is also exposed by attitudes and feelings I have about *me*.

In a message about self-worth, Ruth Myers pointed out that we are always looking into a mirror of some kind for our feelings of self-worth. Usually we peer into the mirror of other people's opinions about us. We are convinced that they're accepting or rejecting us (as indeed some of them are) because of our appearance, performance, or status. But these three factors are like a three-legged stool: If any one of them breaks down, our self-esteem takes a devastating tumble.

As I listened to Ruth, I thought to myself, *What events this week are going to demonstrate the basis of my self-worth?*

Later that week I was to speak to a group of women on the

North Shore of Chicago. For the first time in my life, I developed an infection in my eye. Getting up in front of those women with my eye swollen and half-closed made me feel ugly. As my feelings about myself took a nosedive, I had to acknowledge I was looking into the mirror of people's opinions about my appearance.

A day or so before this occasion, I was driving around the North Shore in a borrowed car, trying to find the home of a friend, the office of the eye doctor, and other places. I kept getting lost, and so I was late to each of my appointments. I chided myself, "Good grief, Carole. Can't you even find your way around a city where you lived for fourteen years?" I was depending on performance for a large part of my self-worth.

And status? Well, I've always been—and felt like it, too—very average. No one really wants to be average. But I was the middle child of a middle-class family living in a middle-sized town in middle America. I wasn't a valedictorian or drum majorette. Never abused by my family. Never been in jail. Just average. As a mother, I didn't even come up to average (which at the time was 2.2 children, I think). God gave us only one (but she's a humdinger).

I prayed, "Oh, Lord, I'm doing it again! I'm looking at how I think people perceive me. I'm focusing on myself, wondering how I look, how I perform, and what my status is. Instead I need to look into the mirror of Your love for me. I know that You love and accept me completely. Help me, Father, to always remember that!"

I find that whenever (and I'm ashamed to tell you that it happens often) I get my eyes off who God is and concentrate on what I am not, I get discouraged.

⑥

Our actions and words expose us, graphically revealing what we're thinking about. And most of the time in the marketplace of life, we display a "me first" philosophy.

From time to time Jack and I have the privilege of sharing a marriage seminar with various groups around the country. One of the points we emphasize is that after God Himself, husbands and wives need to know and feel that they are number one in the thoughts of their spouses.

At one seminar, a husband privately shared this interesting example with us. He and a friend had taken refuge from a storm under a small tree (they thought lightning hit only the big ones) when suddenly lightning struck, traveling down the trunk of the tree and knocking his friend unconscious. It jumped to the metal trim in this man's belt, leaped around his waist, and temporarily paralyzed him from the waist down. As soon as possible, he telephoned his wife from the hospital. "Don't worry, dear," he said, "but I was struck by lightning. I'm in the hospital now." His wife shouted, "Well, what am I supposed to do? The car won't start!"

He told this story with a wry smile that didn't quite reach his eyes. The wife's first thought had been for herself—for her own predicament.

A woman once told me of the death of her husband, and then she added, "The thing I'm having the most difficulty forgetting—forgiving, really—is the time I had to drive myself to the hospital for a hysterectomy because it was my husband's afternoon to play golf." The central concern in that husband's mind was his golf game.

⑥

We are told these days that we have to look out for number one. Brazen voices tell us, "If I don't look out for me, nobody else will!" *My* happiness, *my* ego, and *my* satisfaction head the list of what is supposedly important.

But that's not what God says. He tells us to seek Him and His kingdom *first*. He says that even if we gain the whole world, if we don't have Him, we don't have *anything at all*.

Like a constantly turning prism, reflecting a multitude of colors, so my focus, my mindset, is manifested on the walls of my life in splintered and fractured hues. My attitude about myself and others reveals my focus; my priorities and contentment reflect this same focus.

The focal point of my existence is so vital and important that I must listen carefully to God when He speaks to this issue. And He does speak clearly. He tells me that I am to *set my heart on Him*!

**FOR REFLECTION**

1. Read Psalm 62 and notice the words *only* and *alone*. What needs of ours are met in God alone?
2. What can you do to base your self-worth in God alone?

# CHAPTER EIGHTEEN

# The Measure of Joy

Help Lord . . .
Help Lord . . .
Help Lord . . .

It was an Ephesians 3:20 weekend—all that I could ever have imagined or asked for. God had blessed the conference with a warm, compassionate, exciting group of women, and I almost floated into my in-laws' home, anticipating a boisterous welcome from my loved ones. But the house was empty.

Disappointed, I kicked off my shoes and slung my suitcase on the den hide-a-bed, the balloon of my enthusiasm already pricked. A few minutes later the family breezed in, tired from a weekend of visiting friends in the desert. I got a casual kiss and a "Hi, how'd it go?" before one disappeared into the kitchen, another into the bedroom, and the third—my husband—headed for the phone. The balloon of my enthusiasm went flat. Shreds of self-pity collected at my feet.

Sharing exciting happenings is a natural part of warm relationships. So as soon as Jack was off the phone, he sat down beside me and began to tell me about *his* exciting weekend. I listened, feeling grumpy inside. God gave him some wonderful opportunities to share Christ, some precious new friends, and he described some highlights from a great weekend. I tried to get excited about his excitement. But I still felt grumpy.

Then he was off again to make another phone call. *Okay*, I thought, *if you don't want to hear about what's happened to me, I'll just hibernate.* I went into the den, shut the door, and began to read a book.

My thoughts accused me: *Carole, how could you? God has just blessed both you and Jack in an amazing way, and you're having a dirty rotten attitude. Don't you think you'd better practice what you preach?*

I answered myself, "I don't feel like it! I'm having a private pity party, and I'd just as soon not break it up, thank you."

A voice sounded somewhere within me: "Carole, this weekend you talked about the fact that joy is a choice, right? That 'you don't feel your way into acting, but you act your way into feeling.' Isn't that true?"

"Don't remind me," I countered. "If I choose to act joyfully, then no one will know how terrible I'm really feeling."

"True," came the voice. "But is that more important than obeying Me?"

Just then my silent conversation was interrupted by Jack coming into the den, asking me if there was something wrong. Bless him. He is so sensitive.

And then we did talk. He listened and rejoiced with me. My excitement inflated again from his careful attention.

I never did find out who was going to win—my unreasonable attitude or the still, insistent voice of God. Once again God had provided a "way of escape" for me. But I was reminded once again that I can dwell crushed under the mountain of my problems and my circumstances, or I can choose to consider them joy and then be freed to soar above those very difficulties.

## Growing in Joy

Scripture tells us, "Everyone should be quick to listen, slow to speak and slow to become angry, for man's anger does not bring about the righteous life that God desires" (James 1:19-20). For many years that was not a picture of my life. And there are many times when I fall short of God's standard. But He and I are working on it.

Before I was ready to deal with specific commands on anger, God had to bring me back to the book of James. When you think of the first chapter of James, what do you think of? Suffering, right?

Well, it's about joy. Yes, it really is.

The initial lesson James gives us is that we *choose* whether or not we will live under our problems or above them. We are responsible for our actions. "When all kinds of trials and temptations crowd into your lives, my brothers, don't resent them as intruders, but welcome them as friends! Realize that they come to test your faith and to produce in you the quality of endurance. But let the process go on until that endurance is fully developed, and you will find you have become men of mature character, men of integrity with no weak spots" (James 1:2-4, PH).

That's what I need: the quality of endurance, fully developed, that leads to a mature character. And how is this accomplished? Through trials and temptations. (I don't like it, but that's what it says.) Trials are friends in disguise.

Have you been welcoming any trials lately? I have to admit, that's hard for me to do. How can I actually consider it joy when difficulties invade my life? What can I do to ensure that my life will be full of joy?

God gives several "how-to's" that, if practiced, will fill us with His music to the limit of our capacity. We may hear the strain of the song faintly or perhaps with great reverberation in our ears. It all depends on the amount and depth of our receiving.

God tells us to "consider it joy" when we are faced with difficulties. He commands it. And if He commands it, He will give us the ability to do it. But how?

*God's Word* will fill us with joy. Jesus said to His disciples, "I have told you this so that my joy may be in you and that your joy may be complete [or full]" (John 15:11). Behind that statement are all the precious things He has told us about heaven, abiding in Him, and spiritual fruit. All the wonderful truths He has shared—His very own Word—are bound to fill us with joy.

And it's true. The difference between having a little joy or being filled up with joy lies in how much or how little we are willing to settle for. If we sip shallowly, we will have shallow joy. If we drink deeply, letting His Word quench our spiritual thirst with refreshing water, then we will be filled with joy.

When was the last time you were so filled with joy from reading the promises of God that inside you were jumping up and down and clapping your emotional hands? God wants to flood our hearts with overwhelming joy from His Word. But first we have to ask Him for that joy, beginning with expectancy and then digging for the treasures. We have to be willing to spend the time and energy to dwell richly in His presence.

The story is told of a gifted concert violinist who was complimented after the conclusion of a particularly moving performance.

"That was absolutely wonderful," said the admirer. "I'd give my life to be able to play like that."

"I did," replied the artist.[1]

It takes commitment to be filled with joy.

If we want to consider our trials with a joyful attitude, we must *keep our eyes on the end result*. There is a purpose for all the trials God allows to crowd into our lives. The purpose has to do with a quality of life—a honing of our character, a perfecting of the inner person. If we can see beyond the circumstances to the end results, then joy will ensue. And what results there are! Only one is described in James, but what a fantastic one it is. The testing of our faith develops perseverance; and perseverance, when it has chipped away at us long enough, is going to make us mature—complete. Through this growing process, we will become women of mature character.

In *Discovering God's Will*, a study book by Warren and Ruth Myers, this truth is aptly stated:

> Often we feel we know better than God what is good for us. To some of us, . . . it means getting what we think we want, when we want it. We want what brings a present sense of pleasure, relief, or achievement. God also cares about our present joy, but even more he wants to ripen our capacity for enjoyment in every aspect of our person. He wants us to learn happiness not governed by what happens in our lives; a stable happiness that is not always threatened. He wants us to go beyond the dribbles of satisfaction we can force out of life.[2]

If we *do what God says*, we will have joy. "Blessed [happy] is the man who perseveres under trial, because when he has stood the test, he will receive the crown of life that God has promised to those who love him" (James 1:12).

Maturing through the trial of my temper—persevering by biting my tongue when I feel like unleashing it, counting to ten when I want to explode, disciplining myself by sticking to the conflict instead of digging up the past—has not only helped in my "growing up," but it has given me true joy.

As you consider the importance of being filled with joy, remember that joy is not a feeling (although when you practice choosing joy, a feeling of joy will eventually come). Remember the statement, "You don't feel your way into acting; you act your way into feeling." Exactly. It is true when it comes to love in a marriage; it is true about cheerfulness in the home; it is true about joy in our lives. When we obey *anyhow*, the feeling of joy will follow.

Our joy brings joy to the Father. These are relative measures of joy. But God wants to give us even more than a measure. He wants us to be filled to overflowing, and so again I pray, "Lord, keep showing me how."

### FOR REFLECTION

1. Think about your ability to choose joy in the midst of upsets. Do you choose joy easily, or do you usually prefer a pity party?
2. How can you grow in joy and learn to welcome trials?
3. Do you think it's possible to "act your way into feeling" joy? If so, how can you do that this week?

# CHAPTER NINETEEN

# Filled with Joy and Praise

Help Lord . . .
Help Lord . . .
Help Lord . . .

A small card tacked to my cork penholder reads:

JOY
is the flag flown
from the castle
when the King is in residence!

". . . when the King is in *residence*!" Not a guest in the residence, but *fully occupied* by Him. When our lives are saturated with God, our joy will be full.

I almost came up out of my chair one day when I was reading Proverbs. It had been a rather ordinary day in an ordinary week in an ordinary month. But Proverbs 8:30-31 showed me how an ordinary day can become extraordinary. It read, "I was filled with delight day after day, rejoicing always in his presence, rejoicing in his whole world and delighting in mankind."

In the context, the "I" is Wisdom, which is a picture of Christ. Because Christ lives in me (Galatians 2:20), this passage in Proverbs should be a description of *me*. It says that three things will fill us with delight.

The first focus of our rejoicing is being in *His presence*. We are told to delight in God Himself. If we don't delight in Him, we will be unable to delight in the other two.

In the midst of Job's despair, he glanced back over his shoulder to picture for us the love and blessing of God on his life. Job said, "God watched over me, . . . his lamp shone upon my head and by his light I walked through darkness! . . . God's intimate friendship blessed my house, . . . my path was drenched with cream" (Job 29:2-6).

Don't you love that? "His path was drenched with cream!" How often do you and I feel that way? If not, could it be that we are not sensitive to God's blessings — not looking for them, praying for them? I'm not talking about material blessings, but the riches of His grace.

Our second focus is rejoicing in *His whole world*. I must admit that this isn't hard to do in Colorado Springs. Today is a day I wish I could capture on paper, photocopying about 362 days a year just like it (365 might get a bit monotonous). Deep blue sky, snow-capped Pikes Peak, seventy-degree temperature, crystal clear air. In my walk this morning, I had to spend most of my time just praising God for His world. But even in Colorado — and in spite of God answering my prayer when we moved here, which was, "Lord, help me never to take this beauty for granted" — I often fail to delight in His world. I don't take the time to examine the beauty of the flowers, to observe the sunsets, to wriggle my toes in the grass, to heed the soft music of rain on the leaves, or to appreciate God's deep bass organ of thunder.

God Himself expressed delight in His world, rejoicing in how "the morning stars sang together" and how He had "given order to the morning and shown the dawn its place, that it might take the earth by the edges and shake the wicked out of it" (Job 38:7,12-13).

How long has it been since you delighted in the morning stars while they were singing like a choir? When was the last time you got up expressly to see the dawn being shown its place by God?

Our third focus is *delighting in other people*.

I wonder how many of us divide the people we know into two categories — those we can delight in (grandchildren, for sure!) and those we can't. We usually concentrate our thinking on those we can't.

More and more I'm realizing that God wants me to rejoice in all (well, most) of humankind—certainly in those He has called to be His children. In order to do this, I must practice Philippians 4:8: "Fix your thoughts on what is true and good and right. Think about things that are pure and lovely, and dwell on the fine, good things in others. Think about all you can praise God for and be glad about" (TLB).

It's easy to be negative. In one family survey parents were asked to record how many negative—as opposed to positive—comments they made to their children. Results: They criticized ten times for every favorable comment.

We often think about the negative characteristics in other people or the things they have done to hurt us. The negative things in me (and there are many) often oppress me. But I must remember that I, too, am one of God's special creatures. I need to practice Philippians 4:8 in my thoughts not just about others but also myself.

Thinking about Proverbs 8:30-31, I asked myself, "How often do I deliberately stop the flow of negative thoughts and determine to think only what is true and right and good?" (Answer: Not often enough.) "How often do I delight in others?" (Answer: maybe once a month, if I'm lucky.) Yet this is what wisdom does. This is what Christ does. This is what I, with Christ living in me, should do—and I can, with His strength and help.

## An Act of Will

Joy comes from deliberately choosing, as an act of my will, to delight in God, His world, and His people. Joy also comes from seeing God invade His world and His people through His answers to our cries.

I am convinced that much of our lives is dull and boring instead of full and rewarding because we fail to invite God to become a part of the dailies. God tells us to ask Him. He all but begs us to ask Him—He commands us to ask Him. But we don't. Much of life is lived as though He were not around. Yet Christ promised, "Until now you have not asked for anything in my name. Ask and you will receive and your joy will be complete" (John 16:24).

When I read the bumper sticker—"You are children of God. Please call home"—I grinned and "called home" right on the spot. But I shouldn't need such a reminder to pray *without ceasing*—to continually ask my Father to be involved in the smallest details of my life.

Yes, at times it is work to pray. And again, it is a choice. Our *wills* are involved.

J. Sidlow Baxter makes an excellent point when he says, "Most of us need to lift our prayer life from the tyranny of our moods." He then talks about a time when he had allowed prayer to get crowded out of his life. He would repent, try again, fail, confess, and then the whole process would be repeated. One day he had to face up to his own nature. He recounts this inner struggle in a fascinating allegory.

> I'm not the introspective type, but that morning I took a good look into Sidlow Baxter. And I found that there was an area of me that did not want to pray. I had to admit it. It didn't want to pray. But I looked more closely and I found that there was a part of me that did. The part that didn't was the emotions, and the part that did was the intellect and the will.
>
> Suddenly I found myself asking Sidlow Baxter: "Are you going to let your will be dragged about by your changeful emotions?" And I said to my will: "Will, are you ready for prayer?" And Will said, "Here I am, I'm ready." So I said, "Come on, Will, we will go."
>
> So Will and I set off to pray. But the minute we turned our footsteps to go and pray all my emotions began to talk: "We're not coming, we're not coming, we're not coming." And I said to Will, "Will, can you stick it?" And Will said, "Yes, if you can." So Will and I, we dragged off those wretched emotions and we went to pray, and stayed an hour in prayer.
>
> If you had asked me afterwards, Did you have a good time, do you think I could have said yes? A good time? No, it was a fight all the way.

What I would have done without the companionship of Will, I don't know. In the middle of the most earnest intercessions I suddenly found one of the principal emotions way out on the golf course, playing golf. And I had to run to the golf course and say, "Come back" . . . It was exhausting, but we did it.

The next morning came. I looked at my watch and it was time. I said to Will, "Come on, Will, it's time for prayer." And all the emotions began to pull the other way, and I said, "Will, can you stick it?" And Will said, "Yes, in fact I think I'm stronger after the struggle yesterday morning." So Will and I went in again.

The same thing happened. Rebellious, tumultuous, uncooperative emotions. If you had asked me, "Have you had a good time?" I would have had to tell you with tears, "No, the heavens were like brass. It was a job to concentrate. I had an awful time with the emotions."

This went on for about two-and-a-half weeks. But Will and I stuck it out. Then one morning during that third week I looked at my watch and I said, "Will, it's time for prayer. Are you ready?" And Will said, "Yes, I'm ready." And just as we were going in I heard one of my chief emotions say to the others, "Come on, fellows, there's no use wearing ourselves out: they'll go on whatever we do."

That morning we didn't have any hilarious experience or wonderful visions. . . . But Will and I were able with less distraction to get on with praying. And that went on for another two or three weeks. In fact, Will and I had begun to forget the emotions. . . .

Suddenly one day, while Will and I were pressing our case at the throne of the heavenly glory, one of the chief emotions shouted "Hallelujah!" and all the other emotions suddenly shouted, "Amen!" For the first time the whole territory of James Sidlow Baxter was happily coordinated in the exercise of prayer, and God suddenly became real and heaven was wide open and Christ was there and the Holy Spirit was moving and I knew that all the time God had been listening.[1]

xter's story is my story too. Prayer is work. Of course it
the most joyful, wonderful work that a Christian can be
n. After all, we're talking to the King of kings personally,
on a ᵢₐ‿ to-face basis, because of our forgiveness by the blood of
Jesus Christ.

But human nature being what it is, the world and its temptations being what they are, the pressures of society, the busyness of
our days—these negative factors quite often rob us of the joy of the
act of praying. And that is where Will comes in. And Will needs to
keep coming in until the joy returns—joy first of all in the actual
time we spend praying, and then in God's answers.

Someone asked a Christian, "If I accept your Jesus Christ,
what will happen to me?"

The answer was, "You will stumble upon wonder after wonder,
and every wonder will be true!"[2]

Fullness of joy. Our hearts are to be filled with joy. They are also
to be filled with praise.


## Occupying Our Hearts with God

One morning I wrote:

> Her thoughts said, "You have told me that I should be filled
> with praise. My soul is greatly lacking in gladness. Teach
> me Thy way."
>
> Her Father said, "One of the ways the soul is supplied
> with delight is by seeing Me work in the events of those
> you love. Watch and see."

The day began with small stirrings of sound. I heard voices
murmuring, water running, Gonzo (the dog of fifty-seven vari-
eties) pattering across the tile floor. The small den hide-a-bed
creaked as I stirred. It was 5:30 A.M., and I opened my eyes reluc-
tantly, then came awake, fully alert. I poked my head out of the
red-curtained doorway and inquired, "Is this it?"

Quickly Lynn and her husband Tim replied in unison, "Yes, this
is it!"

I had arrived in quaint Guanajuato, Mexico, two days before, timing my arrival to coincide with Lynn's due date for grandchild number two. Eric, age three, would need watching while Lynn was at the hospital. I'd had thirty-six hours to visit them and to become acquainted with their third-floor apartment before this early hour on May 21.

Shortly after Lynn went into the tiny bathroom, we heard a frantic scream. "Help! The baby's coming! I can't get off the toilet!"

Tim and I rushed in to see Lynn arching her back and hanging on to a towel bar with a desperate grip.

"We can't make it to the doctor's or the hospital!" she wailed.

Tim rushed for the phone. Hastily, he called a friend to go after the doctor, who lived outside the town and didn't have a phone.

Gone were our original plans to pick up Solita, the Lamaze coach, to fetch the doctor, and to journey on to the hospital. In fifteen seconds all our best-laid plans were erased.

"Get a sheet!" yelled Tim, so I grabbed one off the hide-a-bed. "We'll try to get her to the den."

But Lynn couldn't move that ten-foot distance. So Tim eased her to the tile floor of the bathroom, deftly sliding the sheet under her and cushioning her head with a couple of pillows. Because her body blocked the door of the bathroom, I couldn't even get in to hold her head.

Tim was trying to do three things at once — call for help (I can't speak Spanish), hold Lynn's arms while she was having almost constant contractions, and deliver his own child into the world.

Lynn's cries had awakened Eric, who appeared at his bedroom door wide-eyed and frightened. I tried to keep him in his room, but he'd have none of that. He was crying for his daddy (who was very busy at the moment.) Finally, I got him settled on the hide-a-bed, caring also for bewildered Gonzo.

I felt helpless — not even being able to answer the phone for Tim. When it rang, I answered and yelled frantically, "I don't know! Just hurry!"

Tim was magnificent, and Lynn a brave trooper. At one point I peered in to see a tiny crack of blood and flesh emerging. Tim feared that the cord had wrapped itself around the head. But as he gently pushed with his finger he was greatly relieved to find it hard—like a head, not a cord.

I left to tend Eric, boil water, and keep watch at the window for the appearance of the doctor, praying constantly. A scream from Lynn, a cry from Tim, "*Push*, it's coming!" And then I rushed around the corner to see a bloody head emerging, looking dead and somehow not human. I drew in my breath with concern.

Then a thrilling sound—a tiny cry from the baby, even *before* being completely born. The infant was alive!

Lynn gave one final push as Tim turned the baby's shoulder slightly. And then he was shouting and laughing, "It's a girl!" A moment of wild euphoria with Lynn laughing half hysterically but genuinely, "Praise God! It's a girl! It's a girl! Mom, we've got a girl! We've got a baby!"

Tim placed the baby on Lynn's stomach. Just then I looked out the window to see a woman arriving in a car. "Up here!" I shouted. It was a friend, Eva, who was a nurse. She calmly took over and tied the cord with Tim's new shoelaces, cut it with sterilized kitchen shears, and washed the baby with the water I'd boiled (my minor contribution).

Immediately—or so it seemed—the apartment was filled with ten people, including two doctors, one a close friend. In the confusion, Lynn was left alone until she hollered, "Hey, I'm over here!"

Lynn wanted her father to know immediately, so I called Jack at about 7:00 A.M. He said to me later, "I have never heard you sound so *shook*."

Then we managed to get Lynn down two flights of stairs and into the VW van. A friend took Eric for the day. I held the baby as we followed the doctor into downtown Guanajuato.

I was beginning to "come to"—to be less in a state of shock—as we stopped at a hospital you just wouldn't believe: yellow stucco, peeling paint, built flush to the sidewalk; no wheelchairs, no emergency room, no nurses to help. Lynn walked in, and we, stumbling under a load of suitcase, shoulder bag, and baby, tried to help her.

Lynn was helped onto a table in the surgery department. She needed a general anesthetic because she had to be sewn up from tearing both inside and out.

So Tim and I went into the hallway to wait. A man disinfected the floor in continuous slow motion.

This hospital was the closest one to their apartment—a social-ized-medicine government hospital like nothing I'd ever seen before. Green tile walls, green and white linoleum worn to the bare cement in spots, dark narrow hallways. Tim checked out the toilets and said tersely, "Don't go."

No food or beverages were available at the hospital, and there was no place close by to get any. Rusted cabinets containing absolutely nothing stood by each of the six beds in the dormitory-style recovery room—a stark, dark room with one window at the far end. Blood-stained sheets were still on the bed next to Lynn's. There were no pans for patients. Postoperative patients were wheeled in—relatives trailing behind to look out for them. A tiny Indian lady, a long black braid down her back, stood by her uncon-scious daughter who had been injured in a fall. The mother was dressed in an inside-out red sweater over a flowered dress with a bright pink apron. She bent over Lynn's bed for a time, then sat on the floor by her daughter.

A woman squatted on the hall floor, separating tortillas to sell to the nurses. And the cleaning man kept mopping the hall with the strong-smelling disinfectant.

Five uncomfortable straight-back chairs lined the hallway where we waited. For six eternal hours I continued to hug the baby close in my arms, except for a brief time when she was taken to be weighed and footprinted. Tim signed the birth certificate, officially naming her Sonya Marie Westberg.

Finally the doctor came back to release Lynn from the recov-ery room.

At 3:00 P.M. Lynn groggily walked back to the van, and then we rode over the cobblestone streets of Guanajuato once more. Care-fully, Tim helped her walk up the two flights of stairs while I carried Sonya, who was barely eight hours old.

Sixteen incredible hours later, I crawled under the fresh sheets of the hide-a-bed. Our brand-new Sunny was sleeping soundly in her crib. Eric was sprawled on his bed, his blond hair damp on the pillow. Lynn and Tim, heroes of the twentieth century from my viewpoint, were talking quietly in their room.

I smiled into the darkness. Within me a great chorus was singing, "The Lord has done great things for us and we are filled with joy" (Psalm 126:3). The music continued majestically, "From birth I have relied on you; you brought me forth from my mother's womb. I will ever praise you" (Psalm 71:6).

> My heart was filled with
> joy . . .
> > praise . . .
> > > thanksgiving.

Is seeing God operate in the lives of those we love the only way we can be filled with praise? No, for one definition of praise is "occupying your heart with God." But praise encompasses even more than that. Webster's defines it as "an expression of approval: commendation."

Praise, then, goes beyond the *feeling* to an *expression* of the heart. While joy may be inward, praise is an outward expression of a *joyful, inward worship of God Himself.*

### FOR REFLECTION

1. How can you invite God to become part of your "dailies"?
2. Reread the story about J. Sidlow Baxter and his will. What do you learn from this illustration?
3. What are some ways you can "occupy your heart with God" this week?

CHAPTER TWENTY

# Filled with Assurance of Faith

Help Lord . . .
Help Lord . . .
Help Lord . . .

I did a double take and read the ad again.

**SPECIAL PURCHASE**
Authentic, genuine imitation
Gucci-style handbags.
Save 87 1/2%!

The dictionary says that *authentic* refers to something that can be believed or accepted, something trustworthy or reliable.

*Genuine* refers to something that is not counterfeit or artificial.

*Imitation* means an artificial likeness or counterfeit.

Question: How can a handbag be an authentic, genuine imitation? I guess the answer would be by being a trustworthy, reliable, artificial counterfeit.

One cannot have faith in an imitation. Both the faith and the object of that faith must be real. God says that we are to "draw near with a true heart in full assurance of faith. . . . Let us hold fast the profession of our faith without wavering; for he is faithful that promised. . . ." (Hebrews 10:22-23, KJV).

We are to have full assurance. In other words, we are to be filled with faith.

I have some questions about that. I guess the uppermost question in my mind is, "Does the ambivalence of my feelings (being scared, worried, or depressed, for instance) indicate I don't have the full assurance of faith?"

My thoughts turn back . . .

⑥

It was a "whiteout." I was driving alone in a shrieking blizzard, terrified.

The windshield wipers, beating a steady rhythm against the glass, were useless. The beam from the headlights reflecting off the wall of white only added to my blindness, as masses of snow swirled around my car.

Dressed in a white blouse, red wool suit, and heels, I had left the women's retreat just an hour before to drive the 250 miles home to Colorado Springs. As I left the small campground in western Nebraska, the winds were gusting heavily and a bit of rain struck my windshield, but I anticipated no problem on this early October day. I hummed happily to a tape of my favorite songs.

Subconsciously, I realized I had not seen a car on the road for some time, but I ignored the alarm bell ringing in my mind. As the road on this windswept plain tilted upward, quite suddenly the blizzard engulfed me. The narrow road offered no opportunity to turn around even if I could have seen where the pavement ended and the ditch began.

"Please stop the blowing, Father. I can't see!" I yelled aloud.

The wind continued unabated.

"Please keep me on the road, Lord," I pleaded. And miraculously, He did.

I edged along blindly, not daring to stop. My small car hugged the road, staggering over drifts without complaint. For a moment I caught a glimpse of tire tracks on the white ribbon of road ahead of me. Then, just as quickly, they were obliterated by drifts and the falling blasts of furious snow.

Abruptly I came up behind a pickup truck. A man, leaning into the wind and snow, moved in slow motion to my car. He said, "Wait a moment. Then follow that truck. There is a big drift ahead. He'll try to break a path through for you."

In the one moment that I delayed, the truck's taillights disappeared completely, and I was unable to tell where or if he had made it through. Sightless, I crept ahead, praying every minute.

My blue car, plastered white, trudged slowly upward. At last I was at the top of the plateau. A small truck blocked the road, so I came to a stop with no place to go. As the wind died down momentarily, I could make out other vehicles—snowplows, trucks, other cars—many of them half-buried, resting at crazy angles in ditches.

I sat numbly, with a calm not mine, overriding my terror.

Finally a man from the highway department struggled over to my car. As I rolled down my window, a blast of wind and cold air blew in with his voice. "You'd better pull into that church lot," he yelled. "It's warm in the church and other people are there. You will have to wait for a snowplow, and then we will try to caravan you all out of here."

For the next hour we waited, interrupted by the crackling walkie-talkie radios monitoring our plight. "We have two plows stuck here. Need a third," pleaded someone. Then came the answer, "We don't have any more. You're on your own."

A trucker asked me what direction I had come from. When I told him I had driven in from the north, his eyes widened and he said, "How did you get through to here?"

I thought, *I had Help!* but I didn't try to explain. I was the only person who had come from the north in several hours. (No wonder I hadn't seen any cars!) No one else was getting through from that direction.

Two truckers, their rigs almost eclipsing the small church, needed a ride to town. One had decided to desert his truck temporarily after he had almost overturned his rig by braking suddenly for a car stuck sideways on the road. He couldn't see the car until he was almost on top of it.

A plow arrived and the younger trucker agreed to drive my car in the motley caravan. However, if there was a plow up front somewhere, it wasn't doing its job, for our convoy of cars and trucks crested drifts and lost the trail many times. The pickup truck in front of us started to slide. For several moments the driver fought for control, then lost to the ditch on the side. By the time we had offered the occupants a ride (which they declined, deciding to wait for the last truck in our line), the taillights of the caravan had disappeared into the blizzard. We were the first car in the rest of the pack.

The older man, in the rear seat, kept his window cracked to try to see the left side of the road. I watched to the right. Only a giant blank lay ahead.

It was the longest thirty minutes of my life, catching up with that caravan, which was waiting for us at a slightly protected spot in the road.

Kimball, Nebraska! At last! As I was letting the truckers out at a place from which they could telephone, I looked for a motel. But all of them seemed to have "No Vacancy" signs in front. Of course. Everyone was in the same fix I was in.

I finally pulled into the sheltering overhang of one motel entrance, and the kindly proprietor let me use his phone to call the chairman of the retreat I had just attended. I asked her if she knew anyone in Kimball who would put me up for the night. The answer was yes.

The lady who took me in was very gracious. She had no electricity at the moment, but she offered a warm home, a hot supper, a soft bed. Gifts from God, through the kindness of His saints.

As I drove home the next day on a roundabout road that was not closed to traffic, I reflected on the ways of God. He could have changed my route to begin with (I usually fly, but decided it was quicker, in this case, to drive). He could have stopped the wind from blowing or held back the entire storm. But instead of delivering me from the storm, He delivered me through the storm. He showed me His love by providing many Good Samaritans, by keeping me on a road I could not see, by guiding my car steadily through drifts and barriers, by calming my heart even while I was terrified. (Yes, believe it or not, a part of me remained calm the whole time.)

Through the storm. There are many times God delivers us from the storms of life—times of delivery that we're not even aware of, so we never thank Him. But *through* the storm—therein lies the knowledge of what God has done! Therein lies praise to Him and praise for the lessons He can teach us.

Our questions about faith swirl around us, dropping like giant snowflakes on the windshield of our minds, sometimes blinding us to the joy of God that comes through the storms. We cry, "Can we be calm and terrified at the same time and call it faith?"

Friends, it is possible—yes, even probable, and certainly normal—to have totally different emotions at the same time. God understands.

The writer of Psalm 73 accurately describes his feelings. He is obviously upset with the success of the wicked around him. To him they are carefree, healthy, increasing in wealth, and free from the burdens of the common man. He even laments his dedication to keep pure: "Surely in vain have I kept my heart pure; in vain have I washed my hands in innocence" (verse 13).

His wisdom keeps him from venting his feelings to others, but he says it all to God. He confesses that it is oppressive even to try to understand the success of evil men (verse 16).

Then comes the turning point—the key to accepting and understanding the seeming success of evil people. In verse 17 he says that he didn't understand "till I entered the sanctuary of God; then I understood their final destiny." When he entered God's presence he received God's view of the situation.

The only place where we will be able to glimpse life from God's perspective and have real joy in the midst of a cruel and unjust state of affairs is in God's presence. The psalmist at last perceives the final judgment, and he recognizes God's good plan and reality in his life, "Yet I am always with you; you hold me by my right hand. You guide me with your counsel, and afterward you will take me into glory" (verses 23-24).

The climactic statement comes in verse 25: "Whom have I in heaven but you? And earth has nothing I desire besides you." But in the very same breath, he admits confusion and contradiction of emotions. "My flesh and my heart may fail, but God is the strength of my heart and my portion forever" (verse 26).

I'm glad that God includes such passages in His Word. He tells me it's okay—normal, good, fine, natural—to feel several emotions at once. In Psalm 73 we see grief, confusion, despair, and discouragement side by side with trust, hope, confidence, security, and, above all, faith. I relax when I know that an understanding

Creator-Father smiles at the simultaneous diversity of my emotions.

But another serious question blankets the landscape: "Is it possible (even okay) to be concerned without being worried or anxious? Or is *concern* just another word for *anxiety,* and therefore sin?"

I have to admit that as soon as I got to Kimball, Nebraska, I called Jack so that he wouldn't be concerned. (He wasn't—Colorado Springs was absolutely clear!) My point is that I expected Jack's concern for me, and would have been hurt if, after I had been late, he hadn't expressed concern. Is this the same as worry?

Paul says in Philippians 4:6-7, "Do not be anxious [worried] about anything, but in everything, by prayer and petition, with thanksgiving, present your requests to God. And the peace of God, which transcends all understanding, will guard your hearts and your minds in Christ Jesus."

However, Paul himself says, in 2 Corinthians 11:28-29, "Besides everything else, I face daily the pressure of my concern for all the churches. Who is weak, and I do not feel weak? Who is led into sin, and I do not inwardly burn?" Paul was concerned for the welfare of other Christians and for those who were in sin.

To have concern means "to have a relation to or bearing on; to draw in; engage or involve." Only the tertiary meaning is "to cause to feel uneasy or anxious." A synonym for *concern* is *care.*

To worry means "to feel distressed in the mind; be anxious, troubled, or uneasy."

The word *worry* comes from an Old English verb, *wyrgan,* which means "to strangle or injure," with the sense of choking or tearing at the throat with the teeth.

The opposite of worry is "to comfort, solace, soothe, calm." But the opposite of concern is indifference, disregard, carelessness.

We don't want to be indifferent. We do want to be calm. Therefore we must be concerned but not worried.

The answer to my question is that I can and should be concerned, with a godly concern, for the welfare of others. But I must cast my worries on God. First Peter 5:7 says, "You can throw the whole weight of your anxieties upon him, for you are his personal concern" (PH). God is not worried about us, but He is concerned about us! Isn't that great?

Perhaps a warning is needed here, however, for we may use the word *concern* when in reality we are worried, fearful, and lacking in trust in God's care and love. Paul was concerned for people, not situations. We usually worry about situations, sometimes combining them with people. We worry about the loss of a job, ill health, lack of money, losing things—all wrong to do. We are right to be concerned for an alcoholic husband, a hurting friend, a sick child. But it is real cause for celebration to know that God will relieve us of our worries and share our concerns.

I learned a great deal from that snowstorm. I came to understand that although sometimes I have a great diversity of feelings inside, it doesn't necessarily indicate a lack of faith. As I mature, my mind and will should grow more and more compatible with my heart and emotions. I still have a great deal of growing and learning to do as it relates to drawing near to God with a "true heart in full assurance of faith" (Hebrews 10:22). The *Amplified Bible* calls this the "unqualified assurance and absolute conviction engendered by faith."

We know that "faith is being sure of what we hope for and certain of what we do not see" (Hebrews 11:1). Faith is our confidence when we stand on the Rock, Christ Jesus. John Greenleaf Whittier described such confidence:

Nothing before, nothing behind;

The steps of faith

Fall on the seeming void and find The rock beneath.

And then come a trilogy of questions, running something like this: How can I get more faith? Are some answers to prayer blocked by my lack of faith? What produces faith? These are good, honest questions that have to be prayed over and investigated.

Once, while I was mulling over my puny little faith, God led me to Matthew 14:22-33—the story of Christ walking on the water. I carefully noted the reaction of the disciples, especially Peter's response.

When the disciples, who were in a boat on the Sea of Galilee, saw Christ walking on the water, they were all terrified—a natural first reaction to the situation.

Christ didn't give them lecture "number one" on worry. Instead, He reassured them.

Peter then showed a tiny grain of faith by saying, "If (and there was still a good big *if* there) it's you, tell me to come to you on the water."

The Lord said, "Come." So Peter got out of the boat and walked on the water toward Jesus. Peter didn't have a great deal of faith, but as a result of his little faith, he was willing to put himself in a precarious situation. None of the other disciples did that.

Then Peter felt the fierce wind and looked at the towering water. Just as his doubts were growing as high as the waves, he started to sink. His cry for help reverberated over the sea, "Lord, save me!"

Lecture "number two" coming up? Of course not. Immediately Christ reached out His hand and pulled Peter up from the water.

It was only then that the deserved rebuke came: "You of little faith, why did you doubt?" Not a lecture, just a one-sentence reminder.

The response of the disciples, as the Lord and Peter climbed into the boat and the wind ceased, was to worship. They said, "Truly you are the Son of God." Peter had just a little faith, but he acted on that belief.

It is not our great faith but a little faith in action that demonstrates to us God's faithfulness. Who do you think developed more faith in Christ from this incident, Peter or the disciples who stayed in the boat? Of course it was Peter. It was he who walked on the water. And when he began to sink, Christ didn't say, "Too bad, friend. You should have believed more." No, Christ saved him!

Peter learned the lesson best. He discovered that when trouble comes, even though caused by doubt, Christ never fails when we ask for His help. Peter learned that it is not our great faith but our great God who delivers.

Faith grows by knowing and experiencing a faithful God. We get to know Him by beholding Him through His Word, and we experience Him by using the little faith we have to step out on His promises. It's been written,

Whoso draws nigh to God one step
though doubting dim,
God will advance a mile
in blazing light to him.

We have a Father who cares and has given us His Holy Spirit to be our Teacher and Guide. If we are open to Him, He is going to alert us when we worry about our trouble instead of trusting Him. He will assure us that our diversity of feelings in many situations shows not a lack of faith but our own humanity. The Holy Spirit will help us develop the strong, sure faith that comes from knowing a faithful God until eventually we will be filled with the full assurance of faith.

Even in a blizzard.

### FOR REFLECTION

1. How does going *through* the storm build faith?
2. Have you ever had a variety of emotions at once? When?
3. Do you call your worries "concerns"? How can you learn to be concerned without worrying?

# CHAPTER TWENTY-ONE

# Filled with Peace

Help Lord . . .
Help Lord . . .
Help Lord . . .

After taking Jack to the airport rather early in the morning, I braked before turning right on a road that skirts the city. A woman in an old VW paused in front of me, looked to the left (no cars in sight) and then started her right turn. I also glanced to the left (still no cars in sight) and then put my foot on the gas. Looking forward again, I was horrified to discover that the driver in front of me had stopped once more to look to the left. I slammed on my brakes, but it was too late. I rear-ended her small car.

We stood on a street surrounded by large fields without a house or store for blocks. I didn't know what the procedure was in this situation—whether to call the police or not.

Suddenly a voice came, seemingly out of the sky. It was hollow-sounding, distinct, loud. This disembodied voice said, "Do you need help?"

I glanced around, startled. A police car had pulled up about a half-block away, and the policeman was using a bullhorn to ask if we needed assistance. I had to laugh out loud as I gestured for him to come.

I needed help from that policeman. In a similar way, I need help from God in every area of my life—help that He has promised to give. He extends to us the promise of Isaiah 26:3: "You will keep in perfect peace him whose mind is steadfast, because he trusts in you." A few verses later, Isaiah says, "Lord, you establish peace for us; all that we have accomplished you have done for us" (verse 12).

God is constantly asking, "Do you need help?" My answer is always, "Yes. Please!"

Not all Christ-ones have the peace of God referred to in Philippians 4:6-7. Most of us find this peace that transcends all understanding to be a "sometimes" state. It fades in and out at whim of mood, circumstance, and time of day.

Peace is a state of tranquility, quiet, or security . . . freedom from disquieting or oppressive thoughts or emotions . . . harmony in personal relations. It is completeness, oneness, calmness. The opposite of peace is frustration, conflict, hostility.

If part of peace is "harmony in personal relations"—and it is—then forgiveness is not an option for us. Forgiveness is an imperative command.

We will never have God's peace without forgiving people who have hurt or misused us. Never.

We tend to have many false notions about forgiveness. John Hampsch relates a story about such a misconception:

> A woman told me that she urged her angry son to "forgive and forget" when another lad stole his candy bar. So he chased the young culprit, beat him to the ground, sat on him and said, "I forgive you for swiping my candy bar, but it would be easier for me to forget if you'd wipe that chocolate off your mouth!"[1]

Which brings us to the statement, "Well, I can forgive, but I certainly will never forget!" Is this possible—forgiving without forgetting?

John Hampsch goes on to say, "Of course one cannot 'forget' having been robbed, raped, embezzled or insulted. Some hurts in life are emblazoned on our memory ineradicably. But hurtful memories, even though they cannot always be removed, must be 'healed' or detoxified. Paul says (1 Corinthians 13:5), 'Love does not hold grudges and will hardly even notice when others do it wrong' (TLB). . . . To 'forget' such hurts means simply to refuse to mull over them morbidly; it means to prayerfully dispel all bitterness from such thoughts when they arise. . . ."[2]

Lack of forgiveness is sin — insidious sin.

One of the most vital means of maintaining harmony in personal relations — of living in continuous peace — is for us to work at peace among others. "For the kingdom of God is not eating and drinking, but righteousness and peace and joy in the Holy Spirit. . . . So then let us pursue the things which make for peace and the building up of one another. . . . If possible, so far as it depends on you, be at peace with all men. Never take your own revenge, beloved, but leave room for the wrath of God, for it is written, 'Vengeance is Mine, I will repay,' says the Lord" (Romans 14:17,19; 12:18-19, NASB).

Did you get that? *Never* take your own revenge. Now that's a tough one! In many cultures, the "law of vengeance" is deep and unbending. If someone kills or hurts a member of a family, that family is bound by hundreds of years of tradition to kill or hurt someone in the family that committed the wrong.

But let's get practical. Most of us don't live in a culture where a strict "law of vengeance" applies. (And even if we did, God's law stands supreme.) But in our hearts, our old nature cries for that vengeance anyway. We've been hurt, and we long to hurt back. Because this avenging tendency is inherent in our very being, a supernatural attitude is needed to keep us from striking back. Such an attitude comes when God's Spirit dwells in us.

Perhaps you need to take a minute at this point to ask yourself three questions: Am I harboring bitterness against anyone? Am I trying to get back at someone who has hurt or insulted me? Am I failing to work toward harmony and peace with others?

If the answer to any of these questions is yes, please take a few moments to bring that problem to God and ask for His cleansing and healing.

Sin robs us of peace.

Apart from confessing our sin and repenting of it, is there something else we can do to be filled with peace?

Years ago, I memorized Psalm 119:165. I am still amazed at its truth every time I recall it: "Great peace have they which love thy law: and nothing shall offend them" (KJV). When I become offended, upset, or hurt, this verse convicts me, telling me that when my heart is centered in God and His Word, when my focus is on things above, when I am concentrating on what is "right and true and good," then the petty little happenings of my days cannot have that much effect on me.

Staying focused on the Word and on the Lord through His Word is basic to all the "being filled fulls" of Scripture. Romans 8:6 speaks clearly: "The mind set on the flesh is death, but the mind set on the Spirit is life and peace" (NASB).

Another building block toward peace is accepting God's discipline in our lives. "No discipline seems pleasant at the time but painful. Later on, however, it produces a harvest of righteousness and peace for those who have been trained by it" (Hebrews 12:11). When we try to run away from or deny God's discipline, or we turn bitter as the result of it, peace becomes a forgotten factor in our lives.

My peace can be "like a river"—wide, deep, and serene (Isaiah 48:18). It can carry me on to a ripe old age (Proverbs 3:2). Peace is a fruit of the Holy Spirit and part of my inheritance as a believer. But in order to have peace, certain conditions must be met: maintaining a purity of life, working at peace with other people, and keeping my focus on the Prince of Peace. I am to "let peace rule."

The choice is mine.

### FOR REFLECTION

1. What is your usual response when God offers help?
2. Peace includes harmony in our relationships. Are you hindering your experience of God's peace by harboring bitterness toward someone? If so, what steps can you take toward forgiveness?
3. Memorize Psalm 119:165. How can you maintain this perspective?

# CHAPTER TWENTY-TWO

# Filled with the Fruit of Righteousness

*Help Lord . . .*
*Help Lord . . .*
*Help Lord . . .*

When the doorbell rang, though I felt a bit impatient with the interruption in my day, I hurried to answer. My impatience immediately evaporated when I saw Jean, a new member of our Bible study, standing there. She said, "You looked tired at Bible study on Tuesday. I thought I'd just bring this by to you." She handed me a freshly baked, still warm apple pie.

The prayer of Paul in Philippians 1:9-11 came to my mind: "This is my prayer: that your love may abound more and more in knowledge and depth of insight, so that you may be able to discern what is best and may be pure and blameless until the day of Christ, filled with the fruit of righteousness that comes through Jesus Christ—to the glory and praise of God."

I thought, *Jean doesn't know it, but to me she is filled with the fruit of righteousness that comes through Jesus.* Her visit—and that pie—made my day.

I define a friend as one who demonstrates God's goodness and righteousness to me. Being a true friend is part of being filled with the fruit of righteousness. But it is only a part.

To be righteous is to act in a just or fair manner. First John 3:7 focuses on the essence of the matter: "He who does what is right is righteous, just as he [Christ] is righteous." Being righteous means acting like a Christian.

The story is told of Alexander the Great, who was the sole judge of his army. At his command, heads were lopped off and punishment of all kinds doled out. A young soldier who had gone to sleep while on duty was brought before him. Alexander asked him what his name was.

"A-a-a-lexander, sir," the young soldier stammered.

"What did you say your name was?" the commander shouted.

"A-a-a-lexander, sir," the man repeated, terrified.

Alexander the Great got up from his seat and came down and grabbed the soldier by his coat. With their faces inches apart, the commander thundered, "Soldier, either change your behavior or change your name!"

We, as Christ-ones—named after the Lord Jesus Christ— may need to think long and hard about that. Sometimes, if I were sitting in the judgment seat of God, I know I'd thunder to me, "'Christian,' either change your behavior or change your name." (I'm glad God is more patient with me than I would be!)

Righteousness—doing what is right—leads to holiness. We are told to give our bodies "in slavery to righteousness leading to holiness" (Romans 6:19). Righteousness is doing, holiness is being. Righteousness is something you do, holiness is something you become.

Righteousness is the result of God's light in us (Ephesians 5:9), and its results are staggering.

For one thing, the person who is righteous will never be shaken. That is, "he whose walk is blameless and who does what is righteous, who speaks the truth from his heart and has no slander on his tongue, who does his neighbor no wrong . . ." will never be shaken (Psalm 15:2-3).

That's something, isn't it? I'm shaken—or close to being shaken—often.

The other day I turned right on a red light—it's legal in Colorado—without realizing how fast the oncoming traffic was going, especially one very large Chevrolet van. Obviously the driver was upset that I'd pulled into his path. At 50 mph (in a 40 mph zone), he almost hit the rear of my small car before swerving into the other

lane, missing me by a hair's breadth. I could almost hear him saying, "That'll teach her!"

I was close to being shaken that day, not just because of my lack
of "doing what was right" (turning too soon into traffic), but
because of the van driver's lack of doing right as well.

At times I do right but with a wrong attitude.

Lynn was five years old and knew better than to act that way!
Jack was away, and Lynn and I were in church, sitting toward the
front. The sermon had just begun.

The president of the organization where Jack worked sat in the
pew ahead of us, his daughter electing to sit beside Lynn. Lynn
began to talk in an animated way with Jean — out loud.

Annoyed, I glanced at her and said, "Shhhhh."

She continued talking.

"Lynn, be quiet," I commanded in a stern whisper.

It was as though I hadn't spoken.

Angrily, I said, "Lynn, if you don't stop, I'm going to take you
outside and spank you."

I might just as well have been a soft breeze.

Embarrassed, frustrated, mad, I now found myself in the awful
position of having to do what I'd threatened. I took my daughter
firmly by the hand and we left our seats.

An aisle was never so long. In the forever walk down the aisle,
Lynn shrieked steadily, "No, Mommy, no, Mommy, no!"

Outside, I carried out the promised spanking. As I sat in the car,
waiting for her sobs to cease, my own fury abated. It was then that
I heard the inner voice: "Who, then, will spank you for being so
angry?"

I could not respond.

I was not amiss in removing Lynn from church, nor unjust for
disciplining her for disobedience. But I was wrong to punish her
in anger.

How glad I am that God never punishes His children out of
anger, but only out of His great heart of love. His thought is not to
express His disfavor but to teach us to be better people.

I may have done right, but I did it with a wrong attitude, negat-
ing any possible fruit of righteousness.

It was then that I decided to take a good, hard look at the

characteristics of a righteous person. I found that a righteous person will be happy and thankful (Psalm 106:3, 118:19). She will attain real life (Proverbs 11:19) and will be loved in a special way by God (Proverbs 15:9).

Our need is to act rightly with perseverance and steadfastness, for righteousness becomes an armor against Satan, guarding us from his attacks. It gives us a weapon to use against him (Proverbs 13:6, 2 Corinthians 6:7).

Have you ever considered how righteousness guards us?

Blackmailers once sent Charles Spurgeon a letter stating that if he did not place a certain amount of money in a certain place at a certain time, they would publish some things in the newspapers that would defame him and ruin his public ministry. He left at that designated place a letter in reply: "You and your like are requested to publish all you know about me across the heavens."[1] He knew that his life was blameless in the eyes of others, thus they could not touch his character.

Righteousness, like truth, guards our lives against the attacks of Satan. The source of our righteousness is Christ alone. We are credited with His righteousness when we accept Him into our lives (Romans 4:6-8), and when He lives in us, *He* is our righteousness (2 Corinthians 5:21).

If we look through a piece of red glass, everything is red; through blue glass, everything is blue. When we believe in Jesus Christ as our Savior, God looks at us through the Lord Jesus Christ. He sees us in all the white holiness of His Son. Our sins are imputed to the account of Christ, and His righteousness to our account.

Positionally, then, we are righteous in the eyes of God, declared so by God Himself because Christ lives in us. Practically speaking—in this life going on right now, this minute—we are *becomers*. God's purpose is for us to become in this life what He has already declared us to be—righteous. He wants us to do what is right. And that's where the work comes in, doesn't it? My old question surfaces once again. How do we do what is right?

God spells it out.

First, we should hunger for righteousness. Jesus declared, "Blessed are those who hunger and thirst for righteousness, for they will be filled" (Matthew 5:6). There it is again—not only righteousness, but being filled! If we find ourselves not hungering for righteousness, then we need to pray for that hunger. How often in the last month have you asked God to give you an overwhelming desire to be righteous? Begin to pray for it consistently, and then watch what happens.

Second, we should offer ourselves to God, in total surrender of everything we are and have. Ponder Romans 6:13: "Do not offer the parts of your body to sin, as instruments of wickedness, but rather offer yourselves to God, as those who have been brought from death to life; and offer the parts of your body to him as instruments of righteousness." This surrender should be a part of our daily devotional time.

Third, we should obey God's commandments. "Don't you know that when you offer yourselves to someone to obey him as slaves, you are slaves to the one whom you obey—whether you are slaves to sin, which leads to death, or to obedience, which leads to righteousness?" (Romans 6:16; see also John 15:2-8).

Fourth, we should depend on His power. "He who supplies seed to the sower and bread for food will also supply and increase your store of seed and will enlarge the harvest of your righteousness" (2 Corinthians 9:10).

Fifth, we should die to ourselves and put on a new self (Ephesians 4:24, John 12:24). This one isn't easy! (Are any of them?) It is first of all a matter of our wills. Dying to self means dying to pride. And pride is so insidious! Just when I think I've got a handle on it, something else pops up.

There used to be a TV program about a person who could become invisible and visible again at will. He had the ability to make himself either seen or unseen in order to carry out his adventures.

There are times when I feel as if I've unintentionally pressed a wrong button, suddenly rendering me invisible, only I can't find the right switch, words, or formula to make me reappear.

To certain people, I'm simply not there. It's not that I'm either heard or not heard, accepted or rejected, friend or foe, appreciated or not appreciated. I'm just nothing. A blank. A phantom. A nonentity.

I've gone through all kinds of emotions about this sometimes state. Pity. Questions. (Why don't they notice me? Don't they like me? What have I done?) Feelings of inadequacy, hurt, anger. (I'm not going to ask her to lunch anymore until she calls me!)

I'm beginning to realize that I do have a problem. But my problem isn't being invisible. It lies in the reason I so desperately want to be visible to people. My problem is in myself. I want to be noticed. I want Jack to be noticed. I want to be affirmed and appreciated.

I go about this in subtle and not-so-subtle ways. I may make statements like, "I don't think I did that very well," hoping that someone will say, "Oh, that was great." I phrase things—sometimes subconsciously—in a way that pleads for sympathy or recognition.

I need to call this tendency by its real name: *pride*.

This morning God reminded me that "Christ made Himself of no reputation." My NIV says, "He made himself nothing" (Philippians 2:7). And He is to be my example!

How do I make myself nothing? By giving God and others permission to make me invisible. By building up others, not only out loud but also in my own mind. By rejoicing when others are visible and I'm not. By not place-dropping, name-dropping, event-dropping. By knowing that I'm nothing, yet knowing that I'm everything because He lives in me and I am valuable to Him. By being 100 percent concerned with what God thinks of me and unconcerned about what people think. By saying in my heart, "Go ahead, world. Wipe your feet on me!" Wow! That's even hard to write, let alone to feel. I want to get to the place where the important issue is not whether or not the world does wipe its feet on me, but whether my heart's response to whatever God allows in my life is "Hallelujah!"

I'm not there yet. I'm still a becomer. But to me, this is a part of "dying to self." A. W. Tozer, in *The Pursuit of God*, put it this way:

> The meek man is not a human mouse afflicted with a sense of his own inferiority. Rather he may be in his moral life as bold as a lion and as strong as Samson; but he has stopped being fooled about himself.
>
> He has accepted God's estimate of his own life. He knows he is as weak and helpless as God has declared him to be, but paradoxically, he knows at the same time that he is in the sight of God of more importance than angels. In

himself, nothing; in God, everything. That is his motto. He knows well that the world will never see him as God sees him, and he has stopped caring. He rests perfectly content to allow God to place His own values. He will be patient to wait for the day when everything will get its own price tag and real worth will come into its own. Then the righteous shall shine forth in the Kingdom of their Father.[2]

Sixth, we should pray for righteousness and pray for others that they will become righteous. "Open for me the gates of righteousness; I will enter and give thanks to the LORD" (Psalm 118:19). Paul prayed that the Philippians would be "filled with the fruit of righteousness" (Philippians 1:11).

Finally, we should pursue righteousness—go for it, work at it. "But you, man of God, flee from all this, and pursue righteousness, godliness, faith, love, endurance and gentleness" (1 Timothy 6:11).

Sometimes I get discouraged with myself because, with all God has given me, I should be a giant in the faith instead of a pygmy.

> Take a sanguine/phlegmatic woman with godly parents;
> Add Bible-teaching churches, inspiring Christian camps;
> Mix in a Christian college education;
> Combine with a loving, loyal husband who is single-minded in following God;
> Add a child who delights the heart;
> Stir it with years of joys and sorrows, moments of pain and heartache, victories and defeats;
> Then heap in an immeasurable amount of God's grace.

The result of these ingredients should arrive from God's refining oven in the form of a saint like Amy Carmichael or Mother Teresa. Instead, they come out . . . me.

On the other hand,

> Take a woman born into slavery;
> Add a misguided mistress;

Mix in a situation requiring her to have relations with
her mistress's husband and to bear his child;
Stir it with jealousy, disappointment, insecurity.

The result should be a bitter heathen. Instead, out comes the mother of the Arab nations—Hagar—who listened to God and submitted to her stern mistress, Sarah, becoming a significant part of the will of God for the future of the world (see Genesis 16).

I am convinced that I'm not going to be judged for my works in a straight comparison to the works of others. (Fortunately, we Christ-ones will never be judged for our sins—they have forever been buried with Christ—but we *will* be judged by our works.)

Filtered into the data processing of God's great computer, I think, will be all the advantages, blessings, heritage, prayers, and temperaments that each of us have had ladled out to us in the course of life. When the printout appears, it will be a reading of what I should or could have been or done in proportion to what was given to me. "From everyone who has been given much, much will be demanded; and from the one who has been entrusted with much, much more will be asked" (Luke 12:48).

Of course, comparison is fruitless in any case, so it's senseless for me to dwell on what I should or could be, given the various components of my life. My focus must be on obeying God and doing right today.

God wants our lives to be a harvest of righteousness and peace. He wants each of us to be filled with righteousness. So do we.

Let's go for it!

### FOR REFLECTION

1. Think back over the past few weeks. What are some acts of righteousness others have done for you?
2. What are some things you have done for others?
3. Think back to how we achieve righteousness. Which of these steps can you work on this week?

# CHAPTER TWENTY-THREE

# Filled with Light, Overflowing with Hope

Help Lord . . .
Help Lord . . .
Help Lord . . .

She sat two aisles and one booth away from where I stood, unnoticed by most of the ebb and flow of the large booksellers convention. She read quietly, this diminutive woman with wisdom wrinkles lining her face, her turbaned hair coiled in a round bun. Occasionally, a person stopped at her booth, at which point warmth reached out to them and she passed out the books and other literature lining the table before her. I had walked by her cubicle a few times, scarcely noting the modest display, which was dwarfed by the gargantuan booths surrounding hers.

And then a passerby said, "Did you know that Sabina Wurmbrand is here?"

I said, "Sabina Wurmbrand? The wife of Richard, who wrote *Tortured for Christ*?"

"Yes," he replied and nodded toward the unassuming woman a few yards away.

Awed, I turned. No hoopla. No signs announcing who she was or what her life had entailed. No publicity. No "personality booth" for her to autograph books, although she's an author in her own right and the wife of a man who at that very moment was meeting with a group of U.S. senators. No line to stand in as I went to meet her. Just a smile that glowed with the light of Christ, radiating warmth to a fellow believer and sister in the Lord.

That week at the convention I had been privileged to meet senators, outstanding speakers, and celebrities. But the highlight for me was shaking hands with a woman who had suffered imprisonment in a Communist country, separation from her family, torture, poverty, and unbelievable atrocities for the cause of Christ—a woman who, despite and because of all those trials of her faith, remained a humble, untouted, unpublicized saint of God.

In the brief moments we spoke, Sabina exemplified other qualities that we as Christians are to be filled with, and one in particular with which we are to overflow. She was filled with Christ's *light*, filled with *understanding*, and overflowing with *hope*.

### Filled with Christ's Light

Light. The word *light* means "radiance, illumination, brightness, understanding, insight."

In the Sermon on the Mount, the Lord Jesus pulled no punches, clouded no issues. He said clearly, "The eye is the lamp of the body. If your eyes are good, your whole body will be full of light" (Matthew 6:22).

God doesn't want me to have just a little bit of light. He wants me to be *filled* with light. And He even tells me how. "Watch out that the sunshine isn't blotted out. If you are filled with light within, with no dark corners, then your face will be radiant too, as though a floodlight is beamed upon you" (Luke 11:35-36, TLB).

No natural light resides in me. In fact, all was dark until the light of Christ came into my life. Christ declared for the world to hear, "I am the light of the world. Whoever follows me will never walk in darkness, but will have the light of life" (John 8:12).

Mine is reflected light. But that reflected light—"as though a floodlight is beamed upon you"—is to be radiant. Undimmed.

Elizabeth Rooney writes, "The sun has come over the horizon and the eastern side of every leaf and branch and tree trunk is glistening with gold. I feel like that. I'm always the same twig, but to the extent that I allow myself to be suffused with God as the trees are with sunlight I am transformed, golden and glistening. I don't have to do anything except stay in the same place and be still and let him come."[1]

Christ lives within anyone who has accepted Him as Savior. My responsibility, now that I am alive, is to shine—to keep the windows of my soul free from dirt and grime so that His light can shine through clearly.

### Filled with Christ's Understanding

Light illuminates and brings understanding.

Often God's light helps me to understand the purpose of His timing of events, and His working within people. But there is a broader, more comprehensive sense of understanding—an understanding that we are to be full of. Paul writes in Colossians 2:2-3, "My purpose is that they may be encouraged in heart and united in love, so that they may have the full riches of complete understanding, in order that they may know the mystery of God, namely, Christ, in whom are hidden all the treasures of wisdom and knowledge."

"Full riches of complete understanding." Quite an order, isn't it?

The phone rang early one Friday and I left the warmth of my bed to stumble my way to answer. A friend, her voice breaking, detailed a tragic event.

I had really expected the phone call early that morning to be from Jack, who had flown to California to be with his mother after his father had suffered a heart attack following pacemaker surgery. On top of extensive damage to the heart, his hiccups had returned. For three years he had convulsive hiccups that resisted every medication and procedure—a couple weeks with them, a few days without. After three years and a multitude of prayers, the hiccups stopped. Now they had returned, weakening the already worn-out heart of a beloved husband and father.

"Lord, You healed Dad of the hiccups before," I prayed. "Why allow them to return when Dad is so weak? If You want to take him Home to be with You, can't You do it in a more gentle way? I just don't understand."

He whispered to my heart, "You don't have to understand. Only trust."

I argued, "But Lord, You said in Colossians that I should have the full riches of complete understanding."

He answered, "Dear child, you didn't read the whole verse."

I read on then: ". . . may have the full riches of complete understanding, in order that they may know the mystery of God, namely, Christ, in whom are hidden all the treasures of wisdom and knowledge. I tell you this so that no one may deceive you by fine-sounding arguments"—or wrong interpretation!

I sighed and prayed, "Forgive me, Lord. You didn't say that I'd understand everything about events or people or pain. You said that I'd be filled with knowledge about You, and that's all I need, isn't it?"

He answered, "Now you understand."

### Filled with Christ's Hope

Light not only brings understanding, it brings overflowing hope.

I cry inside to see the lack of hope in the world around us. But can you and I truly say of our lives that we are "overflowing with hope"?

On May 7, 1983, I wrote these words:

I sit in my favorite chair. My feet, clad in tennis shoes from my morning walk, [resting] on the matching ottoman. The house is quiet. Only the soft, familiar sounds of the schoolhouse clock ticking above the fireplace and the occasional clicking on of the furnace and refrigerator interrupt the stillness.

It is Saturday morning. Generally when we are in town, Saturday is a "have-breakfast-at-Denny's day" with Jack, then errands, shopping, and a relaxed afternoon watching a golf match on TV. Today Jack is with his mother in California, helping her with his critically ill dad.

I decide the house is too quiet and wonder what I'd do as a widow.

My thoughts go back to the verse I've been contemplating recently: "May the God of hope fill you with all joy and peace as you trust in him, so that you may overflow with hope by the power of the Holy Spirit" (Romans 15:13). I wonder what this really means. Is this a sometimes thing or should it always be present in our lives? What makes us overflow with hope? Hope of what? Am I overflowing with hope right now on this lonely, quiet day?

Suddenly my heart answers. Yes, I am overflowing with hope. Not a "wish-for-pie-in-the-sky" type of hope, but a hope that is born of sureness, expectancy, and life. An "I-know-so" hope.

My hope overflows because I know that if Dad dies, it is only his worn-out body that will be laid in a grave. His spirit will soar and sing so that he will be more vitally alive than he's ever been before. He'll laugh and converse and behold wonders he's never even imagined.

I'm overflowing with that kind of hope.

Job described the magnificence of the stars, moon, clouds, and the sea as merely the outer fringe of God's works (Job 26:14). I overflow with hope—a sure hope—that one day I will see the whole garment in all its splendor and glory.

I think of Joye, of Dad, of Mom, of both grandfathers and grandmothers, and of the many dear friends who reside now in heaven. My heart overflows with hope that I will join them one day.

I think of Jesus—I think of the love of my Lord. My hope overflows with knowing that I'll see Him face-to-face and come into the inheritance He has reserved for me in a place without pain, sorrow, tears, or frustrations. There will be perfect understanding then. I won't wonder anymore why babies die, why nations starve, why people suffer. I will understand.

I am overflowing with hope—even on this quiet, lonely, rather sad day. My Redeemer lives! And because He lives, I too shall live. He Himself *is* Hope. "Christ in you, the hope of glory" (Colossians 1:27).

I love Benjamin De Casseres's definition of hope: "Hope is the gay, skylarking pajamas we wear over yesterday's bruises."[2] I love it—but hope is *so much more than that.*

The opposite of hope is despair. Despair and hope cannot coexist. Our hope is to be in God, in the resurrection of the dead, in the wonderful promises of our Lord. We are to hope in God's glory, in righteousness, in God's calling, in eternal life, and in Christ's return.[3]

Rolling all these "hopes" together, shaking them down into one colossal heap, we would declare, "Base your happiness on your hope in Christ" (Romans 12:12, PH).

The characteristics of hope are vital to our spiritual life. Hope will not disappoint us; it is wrapped up in love; it is an anchor of the soul, sure and steadfast.[4]

We all want hope, both for the joy it produces and for the valuable traits it builds into our lives: joy, peace, boldness of speech and effective ministry, love, steadfastness, encouragement, diligence, and purity of life.[5]

Yes, we all want what hope produces. But some of us may not be willing to pay the price to obtain it. And there is a price for hope.

When we possess hope, we have a responsibility—a great one—in two major areas. We have a responsibility to *share* this hope with others, to be ready to give an answer to everyone who wants to know the reason for the hope within us, in gentleness and reverence (1 Peter 3:15). Furthermore, we have a responsibility to *purify* ourselves. "Everyone who has this hope fixed on Him purifies himself, just as He is pure" (1 John 3:3, NASB).

To meet these responsibilities, we have to first possess this hope in our Lord. And how do we nurture hope until it expands and grows and finally spills over to every part of our lives?

We grow in hope through our *perseverance* and *encouragement from the Scriptures*. Does this sound like a broken record? Our total fulfillment is anchored in this truth. "For everything that was written in the past was written to teach us, so that through endurance and the encouragement of the Scriptures we might have hope" (Romans 15:4).

Reading Job (yes, *Job*) that afternoon when my heart was troubled over my friend's tragedy and the illness of dear Dad gave me true and deep hope. Often I am driven to the Scriptures in discouraging times. And never have I failed to find God's comfort, peace, and hope. This kind of hope may take more than a hurried, "Lord, help." It may take our patient dedication for an hour or two as we pour out our hearts to Him and then wait for Him to speak.

A second way we nurture hope is by *praying* for it. Pray for hope and get others to pray for you. For it is God who gives endurance, encouragement, joy, and peace so that we may "overflow with hope by the power of the Holy Spirit" (Romans 15:13).

A third way we pursue hope comes through *diligence*. Diligence in helping others, in "imitating" those who have gone before us—the saints of old—and in keeping on keeping on.

> God is not unjust; he will not forget your work and the love you have shown him as you have helped his people and continue to help them. We want each of you to show this same diligence to the very end, in order to make your hope sure. We do not want you to become lazy, but to imitate those who through faith and patience inherit what has been promised. (Hebrews 6:10-12)

I was amazed to find out that the word *hope* is used sixteen times in the book of Job. Talk about hanging on!

*Suffering* also produces hope. Read Romans 5:1-5 carefully:

> Therefore, since we have been justified through faith, we have peace with God through our Lord Jesus Christ, through whom we have gained access by faith into this grace in which we now stand. And we rejoice in the hope of the glory of God. Not only so, but we also rejoice in our sufferings, because we know that suffering produces perseverance; perseverance, character; and character, hope. And hope does not disappoint us, because God has poured out his love into our hearts by the Holy Spirit, whom he has given us.

Suffering produces perseverance, perseverance produces character, and character produces hope. Suffering, in a succession of events, then, gives us a solid, far-reaching sense of hope.

A friend of mine wrote the following words explaining the logic in the importance of suffering:

> It has been helpful for me . . . to reflect on the life and ministry of our Lord and to remember . . . there was the cross before the crown. There has to be a battle before there can be a victory. The door to success swings on the hinges of

opposition. Without fail, when we look at the saints of Scripture, we see that conflict precedes blessing.

Joseph—prison preceded prime minister.

Moses—forty years in the wilderness preceded his leading the nation of Israel.

Joshua—war throughout Canaan preceded peace and prosperity.

Job—great physical and emotional conflict preceded unprecedented prosperity.

And on . . . and on . . . and on.[6]

Look around you and see those people who have depth in their lives. They have suffered, which has produced character. And that inner strength of character has produced hope.

Filled with light and understanding. Overflowing with hope. The prize is more than worth the price.

## FOR REFLECTION

1. What can you do today to let God's light into your life?
2. In what do you tend to place your hope?
3. How can you share your hope with others this week?

# CHAPTER TWENTY-FOUR

# Filled with Everything I Need

*Help Lord . . .*
*Help Lord . . .*
*Help Lord . . .*

We sing it. We attest to it. We memorize it. We quote it as our favorite verse. We use it to comfort others. But we don't mean it. Not really.

We declare, "The LORD is my Shepherd, I shall not want" (Psalm 23:1, NASB). Mentally, most of us add a few lines to this verse. Oh, not out loud, but inwardly.

We think, *The Lord is my Shepherd. I shall not want . . . that is, if He gives me a loving husband. And health is a must, of course. I'm sure He wants me to have a caring family, too. And supportive friends. Then I need enough money for a lifestyle to which I'd like to become accustomed. And. . . .* The list goes on and on.

The truth is that we do want the Lord to be our Shepherd. But we're not content without the "pluses." *The Living Bible* gives an interesting rendering of this verse: "Because the Lord is my Shepherd, I have everything I need!" We add in our hearts, "But truthfully, I have several other wants to really make me happy."

Have you ever seriously thought about the statement David made to God in Psalm 145:16? "You open your hand and satisfy the desires of every living thing." Quite a comprehensive, inexhaustible promise, isn't it? This verse seems to be saying that whatever "the desires of every living thing" may be, God will satisfy them.

But does He? What about my friend whose alcoholic husband just left her? What about another dear one with a husband who hasn't supported her in years? What about the couple whose son is deteriorating rapidly with multiple sclerosis? They have desires for a happy marriage, for money enough to meet their needs, and for a strong and healthy son. But God doesn't seem to be filling those desires.

As I was contemplating and questioning this verse, a picture came to mind. (Friends, I don't really have visions — just an active, "sanctified" imagination.) A giant fist came down from heaven. Fascinated, I wondered about all the "good things" it would hold. My imagination ran wild. Slowly the hand opened. There was nothing in it! Nothing but the hand itself.

Then it struck me. This verse doesn't tell me that God is going to satisfy my want for *things*. Rather, it tells me that His character, His presence, He, Himself, is all I need. *God* is my sufficiency.

I looked at Jack sitting a few feet from me on the couch, reading, and I thought, *How I love you! After being married to you nearly thirty-four years, I love you more — much more — than the day we were married. You are such a satisfying husband.* I smiled inwardly and added, *You are just what I need.*

What was I really saying? That Jack has been able through the years to give me all of the material comforts of life? No. Certainly we haven't always had material comforts. That he has always met my emotional needs? No, not always, especially when he had to be away for long periods of time.

What I was really saying was that Jack, as a person, as a man, as a husband and companion, has been and is a person who is deeply satisfying to my heart. He is not perfect, nor am I, but God has fitted Jack to be the one in the world who brings to me great joy, comfort, and stability. His character satisfies me — not *what* he gives me, but *who* he is.

The character of God — who He is — will completely satisfy us if we open ourselves fully to Him. That doesn't mean He doesn't want us to have the "pluses." He wants to delight us with bonuses of every scope and variety. But bonuses, pluses, extras are just additional things. They are not the things that are necessary in order to have joy, peace, hope, understanding, and all the other ingredients with which we are to be filled.

If we are filled full with God Himself, then even joy, peace, and hope are byproducts. They are the result of God in us.

So may our focus be on Him. May our dwelling be in Him. May our strength be through Him. May our joy, peace, hope, and understanding be by Him, until, at last, we are filled to overflowing with God Himself.

## FOR REFLECTION

1. Memorize Psalm 23:1 from *The Living Bible*.
2. List some of your needs. How does God fulfill them?
3. What can you do to continue to be filled and to overflow with God as you face the future?

# Afterword

Help Lord . . .
Help Lord . . .
Help Lord . . .

Wait . . . before you close the pages of this book, pause to reflect with me on what we have just read. If you respond as I do after reading about such thrilling experiences, your heart is full of the hope that your life could be more like Carole's, that you too could see the "little dailies" of your life in the light of His wisdom and use them as stepping-stones to grow more like Him in every way. But I am prone to keep such longings in my thoughts for just a few weeks and then to gradually let them fade and give way to the desires that the next book I read stimulates me to think about.

Carole did not write this book to entertain us or to flaunt herself. The pages of this book are alive with principles that will make a permanent difference in our lives if we apply them.

As I read this book, my mind flooded with memories of the priority Carole has always given to acquiring a knowledge of the Almighty. In the late 1950s — despite the responsibilities of a young child, a household of ten to twelve people, and a growing ministry — she drove two hours every week over the busy Los Angeles freeways so we could meet together to search and discuss the Scriptures.

Note: This afterword appeared in the original edition of *Lord, Teach Me Wisdom*.

In the barren waters of the North Atlantic, only 10 percent of an iceberg is visible. The other 90 percent is underwater. This is true in a sense of Carole's personal life—although she is not cold like an iceberg, but warm, loving, and caring. Her books reflect only 10 percent of her character. Her pen flows freely because her life is 90 percent below the surface, characterized by her dedicated desire and disciplined pursuit to know God in His Word and to understand His workings in her life and in the lives of those around her.

You can develop this quality of life too! The nudges of God you feel in your heart right now don't have to fade. I have always been greatly encouraged by the truth of David's words in Psalm 38:9: "Lord, all my desire is before Thee; and my sighing is not hidden from Thee" (NASB). Paul wrote that "God is at work within you, helping you want to obey Him, and then helping you do what He wants" (Philippians 2:13, TLB). God is waiting right now to be faithful to His promise to give us both the "want to" and the "how to" for us to please Him. God knows both our desires and our defeats, and He has the answers for our questions.

Pause right now and go to Him in prayer. Tell Him all about your longings and desires to be a wise woman. Lay the first brick in the new foundation of your house with an open commitment to make knowing Him—in a personal, in-depth way—the highest priority in your life. Write this date and the decision in the flyleaf of your Bible as a point of reference and a reminder of today's transaction.

Carole illustrates clearly that, like the iceberg, inspiration is only 10 percent of accomplishment and perspiration is the other 90 percent. The goal of being a wise woman is not attained in a magical moment of chance but in applying the knowledge of God to day-by-day living. Every woman is fully aware of the "dailiness" of her responsibilities—dishes, deadlines, dirt, duties, driving, and diet! Do you despair, as I often do, over the barrenness of busyness?

Where in the premeditated schedule of each day is there time for your spiritual growth? Our personal relationship with God can flourish only, as Carole says, through time spent with God in His Word, searching for Him as for hidden treasure, and seeking Him with our whole hearts. Take a minute now and rearrange today to reflect your commitment to being "daily His delight" (Proverbs 8:30, KJV).

Moses told us how to apply God's Word to daily living: "These commandments that I give you today are to be upon your hearts. Impress them on your children. Talk about them when you sit at home and when you walk along the road, when you lie down and when you get up" (Deuteronomy 6:6-7).

But the only commands that do you any good are the ones you know. Deciding on a specific time and place to learn them is in your hands. Before you do anything else, make room for this pursuit in your schedule. Everything must bend for it.

Carole tells us that as we increase our knowledge we gain wisdom. But few houses are built in a day. Experiencing the fruit of scriptural intake is a lifelong process. When we openly commit ourselves and make daily application of God's wisdom, we increasingly enjoy a godly lifestyle.

To my knowledge, the Mayhalls never owned a home of their own until after twenty-four years of marriage. But Carole was effectively building one during those years—she simply didn't have a piece of real estate to put it on! She didn't wait to start her project until she had "arrived" spiritually and circumstances were perfect or until she had a stockpile of materials and know-how. And as each brick was securely cemented into place in her own life, she shared her building secrets with others. As a result, instead of constructing only one house, she has helped put together a whole housing project. This principle was demonstrated in Chicago where Carole began meeting with one woman on a regular basis for "spiritual" building. Soon there were five ladies in the group, and then twenty. Later, Chicago's North Shore had more than five hundred women who met weekly in small Bible study groups that grew from Carole's efforts.

Pick up your trowel, perfect your skill, and watch with thanksgiving what God designs. Even if the cement is not yet dry on the first brick of your house, you can share the truth of it with someone else. By faith ask God today for an apprentice. We are not self-employed builders but "laborers together with Him." We are responsible to the Master Builder, and "He giveth the increase." Paul's attitude in 2 Corinthians 1:24 should be our blueprint: "Not that we lord it over your faith, but are workers with you for your joy; for in your faith you are standing firm" (NASB).

I am convinced that women are capable of having the kind of knowledge, wisdom, and understanding that Carole's book illustrates—if only they will choose to seek it and follow the right path to obtain it.

"Let not the woman with college degrees boast of her intellect; neither let the woman with a charming personality boast of her congeniality; neither let the woman with a career boast of her prestige; neither let the woman with great looks boast of her beauty; neither let the woman with a Christian Dior closet boast of her wardrobe; neither let the woman who has outstanding abilities boast of her accomplishments; neither let the woman who owns a beautiful house boast of her home; neither let the woman who is involved in many clubs boast of her philanthropy; but let her who boasts boast of this alone, that she understands and knows me, that I am the Lord who exercises lovingkindness, judgment, and righteousness in the earth; for in these things I delight" (my paraphrase of Jeremiah 9:23-24).

Marion Foster
Lost Valley Ranch, Colorado

# Notes

Chapter One: Wisdom, Knowledge, and Understanding
1. Hebrews 2:17-18, 4:15.
2. *Reader's Digest Family Word Finder*, p. 834. Used by permission.

Chapter Four: Godly Wisdom
1. See Proverbs 12:18, 15:2, 24:23-24, 28, 30-34.

Chapter Five: Wisdom in Marriage
1. Isaiah 48:17, Psalm 73:24.

Chapter Seven: Thankfulness in Everything
1. Vonette Bright, *For Such a Time As This* (Old Tappan, N.J.: Revell, 1976), p. 54.

Chapter Nine: Pain
1. Joni Eareckson and Steve Estes, *A Step Further* (Grand Rapids, Michigan: Zondervan, 1978), p. 21.
2. Elisabeth Elliot, *Love Has a Price Tag* (Chappaqua, N.Y.: Christian Herald Books, 1979), pp. 60-61.
3. Mrs. Charles E. Cowman, *Streams in the Desert* vol. 2 (Grand Rapids: Michigan, Zondervan, 1966), February 2.

Chapter Twelve: The Tidal Wave
1. Herman Wouk, *War and Remembrance*, in Reader's Digest Condensed Books, vol. 2 (Pleasantville, N.Y.: Reader's Digest Association, 1979), pp. 397-398.

Chapter Fifteen: The God of Sunshine
1. Hope MacDonald, *Discovering the Joy of Obedience* (Grand Rapids, Michigan: Zondervan, 1980), p. 117.

Chapter Sixteen: The God of Delights
1. Mrs. Charles E. Cowman, *Streams in the Desert*, vol. 2 (Grand Rapids, Michigan: Zondervan, 1966), September 29.
2. Cowman, June 18.
3. Amy Carmichael, *His Thoughts Said . . . His Father Said . . .* (Fort Washington, Pennsylvania: Christian Literature Crusade, n.d.), p. 122.

Chapter Eighteen: The Measure of Joy
1. *Reader's Digest*, December 1981.
2. Warren and Ruth Myers, *Discovering God's Will* (Colorado Springs: NavPress, 1980), p. 5.

**Chapter Nineteen: Filled with Joy and Praise**
1. J. Sidlow Baxter, "Will and Emotions," *Decision*, July 1972. Reprinted by permission of J. Sidlow Baxter.
2. Anne Ortland, *Acts of Joanna* (Waco, Tex.: Word Books, 1982), p. 63.

**Chapter Twenty-One: Filled with Peace**
1. John Hampsch, "Reflections on the Gentle Art of Forgiving," *Logos*, May-June 1981, p. 35.
2. Hampsch, p. 35

**Chapter Twenty-Two: Filled with the Fruit of Righteousness**
1. V. Raymond Edman, *The Disciplines of Life* (Eugene, Ore.: Harvest House, reprint 1982), p. 43.
2. A. W. Tozer, *The Pursuit of God* (Harrisburg: Christian Publications, 1948), p. 113.

**Chapter Twenty-Three: Filled with Light, Overflowing with Hope**
1. Elizabeth Rooney, in *Bright Legacy: Portraits of Ten Outstanding Christian Women*, Ann Spangler, ed. (Ann Arbor, Mich.: Servant, 1983), p. 112.
2. Benjamin De Casseres, from "Quotable Quotes," *Reader's Digest*, April 1983, p. 59.
3. Acts 28:15; 1 Peter 1:13; Acts 26:6-7; Romans 8:23, 5:2; Galatians 5:5; Ephesians 1:18; Titus 1:2, 2:13.
4. Romans 5:5; 1 Corinthians 13:7; Hebrews 6:18-20.
5. 1 Peter 1:3; Romans 12:12; 2 Corinthians 3:12; Colossians 1:5; 1 Thessalonians 1:3, 5:11; Hebrews 6:11; 1 John 3:3.
6. Terry Taylor, "Dear Staff Letter," September 1982.

# About the Author

CAROLE and her husband JACK live in Colorado Springs, and are currently serving with the Marriage and Family Ministries of The Navigators. Their daughter Lynn and her husband Tim Westberg also work with The Navigators. Tim and Lynn have two children, Eric and Sonya (Sunny).

Carole grew up in Michigan and graduated from Wheaton College with a degree in Christian education. She is the author of ten books, including *Words That Hurt, Words That Heal*; *When God Whispers*; and, with Jack, *Marriage Takes More Than Love* (all Nav-Press), and has also written numerous articles. Carole is a frequent speaker at conferences and seminars and has ministered with Jack throughout the United States and overseas.

# OTHER BOOKS
## BY
# CAROLE MAYHALL

### WORDS THAT HURT, WORDS THAT HEAL

Words have a power all their own. This book looks at the hurt words
cause through bragging, complaining, gossip, unchecked anger, and
careless remarks and offers alternatives that let words heal.

*Words That Hurt, Words That Heal*
Paperback /$8

### MARRIAGE TAKES MORE THAN LOVE

Marriage is all about choice. Learn how to make choices in your
marriage that are best for all three parties involved—
you, your spouse, and God.

*Marriage Takes More Than Love*
Paperback /$12

### WHEN GOD WHISPERS

This collection of insightful, Scripture-based meditations will encourage you and remind you of God's extraordinary love that He reveals
to us—even in the midst of ordinary days.

*When God Whispers*
Paperback /$8

Available at your local bookstore, or call (800) 366-7788 to order.

NAVPRESS
BRINGING TRUTH TO LIFE
www.navpress.org